CHOICES

Also by Robin Cox

On the wings of an Eagle—A young person's guide to successful living

The Mentoring Spirit of the Teacher—Inspiration, support and guidance for aspiring and practising teacher-mentors

Expanding the Spirit of Mentoring—Simple steps and fun activities for a flourishing peer mentor or peer support program

Nurturing the Spirit of Mentoring—50 fun activities for young people and for peer mentor training

Encouraging the Spirit of Mentoring—50 fun activities for the ongoing training of teacher-mentors, volunteer mentors, student leaders, peer mentors and youth workers

The Spirit of Mentoring—A manual for adult volunteers

Letter 2 a Teen—Becoming the Best I can Be

Making a Difference—The Teacher-Mentor, the Kids and the M.A.D Project

7 Key Qualities of Effective Teachers: Encouragement for Christian Educators

Mentoring Minutes: Weekly Messages to Encourage Anyone Working with Youth

The Barnabas Prayer: Becoming an Encourager in Your Community

The Spirit of Mentoring Series (ebooks):

Over 1000 Strategies, Tips and True Stories, and other resources. Over 325 pages.

Book 1: 167 *Fun Ideas and More Tips and Strategies to Encourage Youth*

Book 2: 160 *More Strategies, Tips and True Stories to Encourage Youth*

Book 3: 234 *Discussion Topics and More Tips and Strategies to Encourage Youth*

Book 4: 60 *New Mentoring Messages to Encourage Youth*
MENTORING: Strategies to Inspire Youth

More information available at www.yess.co.nz

"Cox has managed to distill decades of expert teaching and mentoring into this easily read work. *CHOICES* presents sound wisdom, insights, and strategies for guiding young people through the turmoil of life and the world around them. This exciting book should be compulsory reading for every teacher or pastoral-care worker and every parent who aims to grow happy, significant adults."

—PAUL FLEISCHACK
Senior Deputy Rector, Michaelhouse

"Ken Blanchard, in his book *Lead Like Jesus*, suggests that 'anytime we seek to influence another person we are acting as a leader.' Robin Cox has been that leader for decades. He has influenced countless people, but his passion, because of his story of growing up, is the leadership of youth. This book brings together four decades of experience in influencing young people's lives that has helped thousands to 'achieve greatness.'"

—PAUL BROWNING
author of *Principled: 10 Leadership Practices for Building Trust*

"*CHOICES* is a wonderful collection of stories of personal interactions that Robin has had over a long career. His practical advice, useful questions, and easy-to-read style of writing make this an excellent book for any teacher looking to mentor and guide developing young teenagers."

—TONY REELER
Principal, Bishops Diocesan College, Cape Town, South Africa

"Robin Cox has a wealth of experience gained over many years of successful practice in youth mentoring. His books are always full of hints and practical advice for mentors to follow. *CHOICES* is a sensible, credible, and relevant handbook that provides a wealth of practical approaches for successful youth mentoring."

—BILL GAVIN
former Secondary School Principal,
the New Zealand Youth Mentoring Network

"Making good decisions when faced with possibilities is one of the premier challenges we all face in life. When young people feel appreciated and cared for, they meet challenges and do even better than expected. CHOICES is a tool that provides youth with the ability to probe, question, debate, and feel supported. Through the exercises, trusting relationships are formed that lead to making the best choices."

—Susan G. Weinberger
President, Mentor Consulting Group

"In Robin's succinct and easily approachable CHOICES, he provides a means for those of us who would like to be more effective as mentors to our youth, with a practical way of doing so, based upon latest brain research and a long life of mentoring experience.... He unpacks the theory behind the approach but bolsters this with eminently practical advice that any of us can follow. This book is a distillation, like a precious and rare perfume, of the hard-won lessons in love from a very good man. Read it!"

—Andrew Cook
former Executive Head, Mitchell House

CHOICES

Encouraging Youth to Achieve Greatness

ROBIN COX

RESOURCE *Publications* • Eugene, Oregon

CHOICES
Encouraging Youth to Achieve Greatness

Copyright © 2021 Robin Cox. All rights reserved. Except for brief quotations in critical publications or reviews, no part of this book may be reproduced in any manner without prior written permission from the publisher. Write: Permissions, Wipf and Stock Publishers, 199 W. 8th Ave., Suite 3, Eugene, OR 97401.

Resource Publications
An Imprint of Wipf and Stock Publishers
199 W. 8th Ave., Suite 3
Eugene, OR 97401

www.wipfandstock.com

PAPERBACK ISBN: 978-1-6667-2458-5
HARDCOVER ISBN: 978-1-6667-2029-7
EBOOK ISBN: 978-1-6667-2030-3

AUGUST 30, 2021

Contents

Preface | *vii*

Chapter 1   Catching the Vision—My Awakening | 1

Chapter 2   The CHOICES Framework? | 13

Chapter 3   Peter's Story: Our Choices Define Us | 20

Chapter 4   Clear Goals | 34

Chapter 5   Hobbies and Interests | 48

Chapter 6   Organization | 61

Chapter 7   Interdependence | 74

Chapter 8   Consistency | 92

Chapter 9   Exercise | 104

Chapter 10   Service | 119

Chapter 11   Concluding Thoughts: Make Sense of Confusion | 131

Appendix 1   Mentoring Matters | 145

Appendix 2   10 Habits to Reach My Potential | 147

Appendix 3   168 More Conversations 2 Connect Topics | 149

Acknowledgments | 165

Bibliography | 167

Preface

I BEGAN WRITING THIS book in 2016 as a result of a question my anaesthetist asked me shortly before I was wheeled into the operating theatre to undergo a minor knee operation: "How did you deal with it?"

"It" was my journey through adolescence coming to terms with my cancer diagnosis at the age of nine, extensive radiation treatment and two major operations.

"How did you deal with it?"

I had never considered a question like this. As I reflected, I came to a deeper understanding of how my family, friends, teachers and coaches had moved alongside a struggling boy who lacked self-confidence and self-belief, and inspired and guided him to "achieve greatness", or to reach *his* potential, a journey that continues to this day. And, most of these people displayed the spirit of mentoring without probably even realizing this.

After I retired in 2017, I collated all my teaching, coaching, leadership and mentoring resources, reflected on my experiences guiding over 1000 students in one-to-one relationships—one of my life passions—and continued to develop the content for this book. I unearthed notes and cards from students with whom I had interacted, some of whose stories are shared in this book to give credibility and practical meaning to the CHOICES framework.

My aim is to encourage *anyone* working with youth to consider adapting a proven CHOICES framework I have developed over my forty-five-year education career, so they can motivate and inspire these young people to achieve greatness. No matter what their personal or socio-economic situation might be, most young people can discover the meaning and purpose of life with a significant and authentic adult—a non-judgmental cheerleader—alongside them.

This user-friendly book contains many proven tips, strategies and true stories—names of students have been changed to protect their privacy—linked to recent adolescent brain research which adds greater credibility to the key elements within the CHOICES framework. Repetition is deliberate.

There is a multitude of brain research referenced throughout this book in support of the CHOICES framework, though I must quickly include a disclaimer, as I do not have the space in these pages to provide more detail. I am not claiming to do true justice to the depth of available brain research. Neuroscientist Dr. Francis Jensen places things in perspective: "Despite the great advances in neuroscience, what we still don't know about the human brain dwarfs what we do know."[1]

Through my interactions with youth, I discovered how much they enjoy discussing how their brains develop. Try not to become overwhelmed by some of the brain research shared in this book. Rather, allow it to help you gain a deeper understanding of youth behavior in response to the variety of challenges they face. Think of all this information as providing useful reference points to revisit whenever you wish to do so.

As I continue to reflect on my adolescent experiences, I increasingly appreciate how the life lessons from this challenging season of my life have positively impacted the development of the CHOICES framework.

Topics like the importance of setting clear goals, following hobbies and interests, and living a healthy and balanced lifestyle are explored. I share research to show how the brain is wired for relationships and responds to life situations. Some effective

---

1. Jensen. *The Teenage Brain*.

Preface

communication strategies, ideas on how to develop resiliency, and thoughts about the power of storytelling are outlined.

I suggest the importance of asking "discovery questions" which open our minds to the power of curiosity—to explore new avenues of thought—and the possibility of changing our views as we listen and learn.[2]

Indeed, what do we hear when we take the time to listen closely to what adolescents (and young adults) want?

My research over many years suggests that *all* young people want:

- to be cared for (loved)
- to be valued
- to know that life has meaning and purpose (Appendix 1)

The CHOICES framework embraces the "spirit of mentoring" and provides tips and strategies to help anyone working with youth to respond to their needs. The mentoring heart gives youth the keys to reach their potential within a safe and secure environment.

The CHOICES framework has been woven into all the mentor training I have undertaken. I observed many mentors of young people successfully adapting this framework in the relationships they developed with youth within and outside of an education environment.

My hope is that whether you are a parent, coach, teacher, mentor, relative, or youth worker, you consider adapting the CHOICES framework when you move alongside youth.

We have the spirit of mentoring within. "5 spirit of mentoring tips and strategies" which I have collated from the work of global educators and youth mentoring experts, and most of which can be adapted for any relationship with youth, are shared at the end of each chapter.

---

2. Glaser. *Conversational Intelligence.*

PREFACE

You will also find "Conversations 2 Connect"—ideas to create positive discussions in our interactions with youth, which will build trust when used in a non-judgmental and supportive way.

The pandemic and post-pandemic seasons will highlight the importance of meaningful face-to-face *relationships* between young people and significant adults. This book provides proven strategies to become a positive voice in the life of a young person, even to enhance the quality of teaching, parenting, mentoring, and coaching during the challenging times ahead.

Chapter 1

Catching the Vision— My Awakening

Success is peace of mind, which is a direct result of self-satisfaction in knowing you made the effort to become the best of which you are capable.

JOHN WOODEN

WHAT LIFE LESSONS CAN you share with youth?

How would you explain the term "achieve greatness", and the word "success" to an adolescent?

Who have been the most important positive influences in your life to date?

Who were the most positive influencers during your journey through adolescence to become a young adult? Why this person or these people?

How did your adolescent experiences shape your future?

So many questions to remind us of our uniqueness and how we each have a personal story to share which continues to shape our life experiences.

CHOICES

Welcome to an introductory journey as I share my passion to encourage youth to reach their potential. One of the most important life lessons I have learnt is that, when I choose learning for life, I lead a life of significance. Let me explain this by way of a true story.

Diagnosis

At the age of nine I was diagnosed with cancer of the jaw. My parents initially thought I had mumps. When the swelling did not go down, I was sent to a specialist. A biopsy followed. My parents were informed that I had bone cancer—with a five per cent chance of survival—and would require radiation therapy. The worst-case scenario was that I probably only had two years to live.

I missed more than a term of school while I underwent the radiation therapy, followed by my first major operation. My mother took me to Groote Schuur Hospital in Cape Town, South Africa—later to become famous as the venue for the first heart transplant—every day for two months. I found out some years later that I received two-and-a-half-times the adult dose of radiation as the doctors were so concerned that the cancer would spread through my body.

Success or failure?

Radiation therapy made me tired, and I had to take things carefully. However, I still remained passionate about cricket. I lived and breathed the game. I had made my debut in the school's under 9A team, which I also captained in some matches. Waking up on a Saturday morning, opening my bedroom shutters and checking the weather, remains a vivid memory. All I wanted to do was play because I had a dream to play for my country. My top score was twenty-seven runs, which, to a nine-year-old, was like scoring a century.

While I was undergoing the radiation therapy, I placed a ball in an old sock tied to a beam on the back deck and practiced my batting for hours and hours. I imagined batting for my country and scoring all those runs. My dream was real.

After the radiation therapy was completed, the swelling had reduced. The doctors decided to operate and remove what was left of the tumor. During the next couple of years, I had two fairly major operations, the first to remove the cancerous jawbone and some lymph nodes, the second to graft a rib which would grow as my new jawbone. The hope was that, once I had stopped growing and my face had adapted to this new jawbone, I would be as near normal in looks as was possible, and the final plastic surgery would cover the hollow in my cheek as a result of the first operation.

During the next few years, through to the end of high school, I made regular trips to the outpatient clinic at the hospital, my significant memory being the healing hands of the amazing specialists who treated me as they checked my progress.

I recall the day I returned to school after my first major operation. I sat in the car until after Assembly. The headmaster told the school that I was returning, was disfigured, yet needed to be treated normally.

Many of my teachers reached out, encouraged and moved alongside me in different ways, and at different times. Their acts of kindness impacted my life in a significant way, so much so that I decided, at about eleven years of age, that I would one day become a teacher.

Tragedy brings changes

One occasion during my junior school years, which I remember as though it was only yesterday, was the day my headmaster called me out of class before lunch to tell me that my father was coming to fetch my brother and me. My mother had undergone an operation and was in hospital. My father had been called to the hospital early that morning. As we clambered into the car, my father informed us that my mother had died from a pulmonary embolism.

CHOICES

The family understandably took time to adapt to my mother's death. I was allowed to play sport again after many tantrums and bucketloads of tears had been shed. Through my involvement in sport, I discovered that I had some talent. This awareness probably helped me develop a way to cope with my disfigurement.

About eighteen months after my mother died, my father married again. My stepmother was a divorcee who had suffered the tragedy of losing her son, the same age as me, though in another class at my school. He was hit by a car as he ran across a busy road to watch a helicopter landing on a large common close to a children's hospital. He was blind in one eye, so failed to see an approaching car. My step-sister was a couple of years younger than me.

This marriage changed the dynamics within our family. My teenage brother and sister battled to accept two new people into the family. No matter how hard she tried, my stepmother could never replace my mother. It took her a long time to understand this.

Looking for meaning and purpose

I journeyed through the confusing adolescent years lacking in self-confidence. I had to tolerate the never-ending stares of young and old to remind me of my disfigurement, and was subjected to occasional hurtful comments from my peers. I was shy and a bit of an introvert within a family experiencing what can only be described as "interesting dynamics".

My love of sport, as already mentioned, kept me going. I also joined a youth group for a while, following my brother there. The other members of the group were at other schools and knew each other. Cliques were already formed. I was unable to break into any of these (not that I tried that hard), felt awkward and isolated, and eventually stopped attending. Positive and negative peer pressure was a reality in my life and caused much confusion.

I went through a phase of acting the class clown. I had a great sense of humor, which helped me through some of the challenges of my teenage years. I made silly comments in class and probably annoyed most of my teachers. I did not realize at the time that this behavior was probably nothing more than attention-seeking.

I became a loner for a while and concluded that, because I was different from everyone else, I had to prove myself. In addition to playing cricket at the highest level for my age, I started cross-country running, and soon realized that I had some talent. I set some personal goals and made many sacrifices, trained hard and, because I didn't initially see it as a team sport, enjoyed the solitude of hill training and running in the local mountains of the Cape. I became supremely fit and was selected for the state under fifteen cross-country team, and the state under-sixteen cricket team.

During my final years at school, I moved away from cross-country and played squash, badminton, field hockey and, of course, cricket. I represented my school first teams in all these sports, captained the cricket team, and gained the respect of both peers and teachers, which had been one of my goals. I did not want people to feel sorry for me because of my physical disability, and I don't think they did.

My mentors

My cricket coaches and one hockey coach, in particular, became my mentors. One of these coaches was my headmaster, himself a former international cricketer. I was like a sponge when I was with these people, forever asking questions and wanting to learn more and more. I didn't realize at the time how they were shaping my character and helping me form a value base on which I would build the rest of my life. I was appointed school captain (head student) in my final year. My headmaster taught me so much about selfless leadership, the importance of standing up and being counted, leading by example, persevering through tough times, and never quitting.

During that year I was selected for my state under-nineteen hockey team, and as vice-captain of my state under-nineteen cricket team. I became more self-confident and resilient as the months went by.

After returning from a successful under-nineteen interstate cricket tournament, I underwent my final plastic surgery operation to complete the rebuilding of my face, after which I headed off to university to get my teaching qualifications.

Challenges and tough decisions—a period of transformation

Space does not allow me to share more of my personal story which also has contributed to the development of the CHOICES framework. These topics include:

- how I discovered at the age of seventeen for the first time that I had had cancer as a young boy—which many might find surprising—and the impact that life-changing moment had on my future life choices. These were the days before all the cancer fundraising campaigns and television coverage we experience today. Indeed, we did not have television at that time in South Africa;
- making the tough decision—aged nineteen—to stop playing competitive sport because of the risks involved, and how I converted those sport goals to coaching goals, all of which I achieved;
- a fascinating teaching career that took me to Zimbabwe, other regions in southern Africa, New Zealand and Australia, speaking at an international conference in Jamaica, studying at Fordham University, U.S.A., and being awarded a Churchill Fellowship which allowed me to visit twenty-three youth mentoring programs in Canada and the U.S.A.;
- sixteen years as a school principal and assistant head of a school;
- developing youth mentor and peer mentor programs in three countries, and how, by chance, I became an author.

Lessons from the cancer journey

Ten of the key life lessons I learnt from my adolescent experiences which have significantly impacted the development of the CHOICES framework include:

1. Find people who believe in me and see the potential which I may not always see to be my cheerleaders.

2. Learn how to set and chase *my* personal best goals; enjoy the triumph of hard work. I can achieve my dreams with self-discipline, perseverance and commitment.

3. If I want to fulfil my potential, I must continually improve myself, which includes taking responsibility for my actions and choices, not fearing failure, and learning from my mistakes; believing in myself, backing myself, and practicing humility.

4. Understand the importance of a strong work ethic—to appreciate how important it is to set my sights high and *never* to accept second-best, never to fear failure, or to be a stand-out in the crowd. These experiences are worth the pain and suffering I have to deal with at times to stay true to myself.

5. My attitude defines my progress; how I think affects how I feel, which in turn influences my choices and behavior.

6. Asking for help and learning to be vulnerable is a strength and not a weakness; I am not helpless—there is always something I can choose to do.

7. Wake up each day and be thankful for the opportunities I have to spread a message of hope in a struggling world; support the underdog, the hurting and the broken because I have been there and can empathize.

8. Use my God-given gift of encouragement to make a small difference in the world, especially in my interactions with teenagers and fellow educators.

9. The importance and power of teamwork—when a group of people unite behind an agreed vision and work hard to attain it, I am at my happiest.
10. Retain a healthy sense of humor, which includes the importance of laughing at myself; *how* I think is more important than what I think.

There are two further key lessons I learnt from my adolescent experiences. Firstly, the *choices* I make, particularly about my attitude to life, define who I become. I choose how I react to all that's going on around me. When I choose to carry hope with me at *all* times, I have a greater opportunity to reach my potential.

Secondly, when I focus on being myself, chase my personal best goals and dreams, and no longer try to please the crowd, my life gains significant meaning and purpose, and I have peace of mind. I came to a deeper understanding of what it means to "achieve greatness", or to fulfil my potential. It took me a few years to understand what this meant in reality.

Achieve greatness

We guide young people to achieve personal greatness as they strive to reach *their* potential. This is not about somehow becoming a celebrity with a significant global following, more interested in fame and fortune than being authentic.

It involves reflecting on the culture and experiences of every young person we move alongside. Some, for example, are significantly impacted by the behavior of their peers, the world and expectations of their parents, the world of their faith journey, and the world of working to supplement the family income.

Nor does personal greatness have anything to do with fulfilling other people's expectations to be successful by achieving high marks, or a top job, or being selected for a top team.

As mentioned earlier, I had to learn the meaning of achieving greatness for myself. Put simply: I strive to become the best person I can be. I am fulfilling *my* potential—a lifelong journey in reality.

Catching the Vision — My Awakening

Indeed, author and educator Leo Buscaglia warned: "The easiest thing to be in the world is you. The most difficult thing to be is what other people want you to be. Don't let them put you in that position."[1]

A definition of success from legendary teacher and basketball coach John Wooden, which I have shared with many young people, has inspired me for many years. Reflect on it again: "Success is peace of mind, which is a direct result of self-satisfaction in knowing you made the effort to become the best of which you are capable."[2] I encourage youth to take ownership of the quote and at the end of every day to ask themselves, "Have I done my best today?" If they have done so, they can rest well. If not, what are the lessons they have learnt to work on the next day? They appreciate that they are on a journey to achieve greatness, one that takes time, so they need to be patient and kind to themselves.

Wooden explained his definition of success:

> You have little say over how big or how strong or how smart or how rich someone else may be. You do have, at least you *should* have, control of yourself and the effort you give toward bringing out your best in whatever you are doing. This effort must be total, and when it is, I believe you have achieved personal success. The concept that success is mine when I work my hardest to become my best, and that I alone determine whether I do so, became central to my life and affected me in a most profound manner.[3]

The interactions between a caring adult and a growing adolescent are much like the connections forming in the adolescent brain, as we shall see in the pages of this book. The more an adolescent has a diversity of positive experiences, the stronger the connections formed in the neural pathways of the brain. The more connections the brain has, the more it can withstand and create.

---

1. Buscaglia. *Brainy Quote.*
2. Wooden. *Wooden,* 94.
3. Wooden. *Wooden* 52.

CHOICES

The connections between adolescents and adults who unconditionally love and care for them work the same way. The more we make, reinforce and recreate connections between our youth and the significant others in their lives, the greater the chance our young people have to sprout their wings and fly. My adolescent life experiences are, indeed, proof of this.

5 SPIRIT OF MENTORING TIPS AND STRATEGIES

1. Every young person is unique, with their own story. Allow time to hear their story—listen with a genuine interest as they share and, as the relationship moves to deeper levels, they will feel more confident to share deeper thoughts. Be patient and avoid probing for more information.
2. Mentoring relationships blossom when *trust* is established. Display the qualities of friendship, though never try and become a young person's "best friend".
3. Mentors are positive role-models—"show, don't tell." The journey involves a young person becoming the best person they can be—*their* dreams; *their* goals.
4. Great mentors are respectful and empathetic. They ask questions like: "What do you think?" "What do you want to talk about?" "What is on your mind?"
5. Focus on establishing a bond with a young person, a feeling of attachment, a sense of equality, and the mutual enjoyment of shared time.[4]

CONVERSATIONS 2 CONNECT

Social psychologist and educator Helen Street explains that youth have a greater chance to reach their potential when they have at least one significant adult to guide them: "By helping kids to feel

---

4. Garringer and Jucovy. *Building relationships.*

connected to you and to their world, you are helping them to feel a sense of belonging which is paramount to wellbeing and the ability to engage in learning."[5]

So, how can a significant adult positively connect with a young person?

Most of these discussion topics can be used at any point in a relationship with a young person, though continually remind yourself how social media impacts the lives of youth in a variety of ways. Many of our youth, for example, fail to grasp body language and its importance in building meaningful relationships. A significant adult can model *how* to communicate effectively.

I came across some helpful tips on how to communicate effectively using a SOLER method, though am unsure who pioneered this helpful term.

> S—sit squarely.
> O—open posture (no crossed legs or hands or folded arms).
> L—lean forward
> E—eye contact (when culturally appropriate).
> R—rephrasing (paraphrasing back to the speaker what you think you have heard as you seek clarification).

Here are some non-threatening topics to make positive connections with youth.

1. In what ways can I help, support, or encourage you?
2. If you were trapped on a desert island and could pick one famous person (living or dead) to join you, who would you choose?
3. Imagine you were given a free ticket to visit any place in the world. Where would you visit and why?
4. What is the funniest movie you have ever seen? What happened?
5. What cultural values, types of behavior, and other aspects of your culture should I be aware of?

---

5. Street and Porter. *Better than OK*, 39.

CHOICES

6. How important do you feel cell (mobile) phones are in people's lives? Do you think they help to build meaningful relationships?

7. You are allowed to set one family rule. What would your rule be? Why?

Chapter 2

The CHOICES Framework?

> Growing up is about growing away, about finding an identity distinct from your family. But few teens have a strong enough sense of self to stand alone. It is why friends are so important; together you form a collective identity from which you gather strength and a sense of belonging. And your clothes, music, and friends announce their identity.
>
> Mia Fontaine (15)[1]

IN RECENT YEARS NEUROSCIENCE has revealed how the teenage brain develops in some unexpected ways. The brain experiences significant changes and, with this ever-increasing knowledge, we can look at our unique and talented youth in a new light, as they make possibly life defining choices.

Well-known clinical psychiatrist Daniel Siegel states:

> Adolescent years are filled with a sense of uncertainty by nature.... It's a time of great transition. We move from the relative safety and familiarity of the home nest to a

---

1. Fontaine. *Comeback.*

temporary period—one that may last decades—of having no real home base, or losing the familiar and safe, and gaining the unfamiliar and dangerous. . . . The only certainty in life is change. Therefore, our challenge is to work out ways of supporting adolescents, whilst also allowing them to find their own voices.[2]

And, Francis Jensen reminds us why most young people need and value our support. "Teenagers may look like adults, they may even think like adults in many ways, and their ability to learn is staggering, but knowing what teenagers are unable to do—what their cognitive, emotional and behavioral limitations are—is critically important."[3]

The CHOICES framework explained

The CHOICES framework has been formulated from my research and personal experiences over many years.

There are some fundamental CHOICES youth can make, preferably with the support of a significant adult, within a safe and secure environment. Personal growth takes place, life skills are learnt, and youth make giant strides to become the best and most resilient people they can become as they strive to reach their potential.

When I reflect on my life journey, there were at least three key questions I was answering during my challenging teenage and young adult years.

1. Where do I want to go?
2. Where do I want to be?
3. What do I want to do?

These questions can lead to positive discussions with the young people with whom we interact and introduce to the CHOICES framework.

2. Siegel. *Brainstorm*, 28.
3. Jensen. *The Teenage Brain*.

The CHOICES Framework?

I took the word CHOICES and used these letters to create a framework of seven key elements on which every young person can focus, and which we can use when we move alongside and guide them to live healthy and balanced lives. Instead of youth saying, "I want to . . . ", they say, "I choose to . . . ", a statement that automatically changes their mindset—think: meaning, purpose, action steps, ownership, creative problem solving, entrepreneurial thinking, initiative, positive self-talk, and accountability.

The seven key elements within the CHOICES framework are:

1. Clear goals
2. Hobbies and Interests
3. Organization
4. Interdependence
5. Consistency
6. Exercise
7. Service

Understanding the adolescent brain— transforming relationships

As we develop our understanding of the teenage brain from more and more research, and apply the CHOICES framework, the significance of our supportive role in the lives of youth can be more clearly understood.

The term "neural plasticity" refers to the brain's ability to change as a result of experience and interaction with the environment. The brain grows and adapts in response to external stimuli, so it is malleable like plastic. This is why adolescence is a time of great risk, yet also great opportunity.

The brain changes during adolescence and loses what it doesn't use. When youth experience a holistic education—development of the "whole" person—they can truly discover, shape, refine, nurture, and develop their unique gifts and talents. With the support of significant adults in their lives, especially their parents and teachers, they can learn how to chase their dreams and reach for the stars.

Author and brain researcher Nicola Morgan encourages us to think of our brain cells and connections as being like trees.[4] So, imagine starting with a young tree with a few branches. If you water, feed and nourish the tree, and the climate is right, it will grow many branches. Similarly, when we practice something, it develops the brain cells which are responsible for that particular learning experience. More branches are grown and they become stronger, hence the importance of more practice, an important life learning tip for anyone working with youth—practice makes permanent.

After significant brain growth just before and at the start of puberty, there is a time during adolescence when the branches are cut back and pruned—a bit like pruning a tree to make its branches fewer, yet thicker and stronger.

Francis Jensen explains:

> The process of fine-tuning and turning off neuronal connections that may have been made in childhood but are no longer needed is called pruning and it accelerates during mid-to late adolescence when unneeded synapses [neurons communicate with one another at junctions called synapses] are removed.[5]

With all this activity taking place in the adolescent brain, Daniel Siegel believes that the most dangerous times of our lives are between the ages of twelve and twenty-four.

A developing muscle

We can share the idea with youth that the brain is like a muscle which gets stronger as we use it. As we promote mindfulness—a deliberate inner awareness of what one is thinking, feeling and

---

4. Morgan. *Blame My Brain*.
5. Jensen. *The Teenage Brain*.

experiencing—we also encourage our young people to identify and further develop their strengths to become more resilient.

Linda Lantieri, internationally renowned expert in social and emotional learning and conflict resolution, states: "Resilience is the ability to successfully manage life and adapt to stressful events . . . building resilience is about integrating what's happening by having support, safety and love around the child."[6]

Stanford University psychologist Carol Dweck's research over thirty years led her to believe that the most motivated and resilient students are those who believe that their abilities can be developed through their effort and learning. Therefore, she suggests that it matters greatly what students believe about their intelligence. Intelligence is not a matter of *being* smart but of *becoming* smart. This is a lifelong journey and further underlines the non-judgmental and caring roles of the significant adults in every young person's life.

Throughout life we make choices about what we eat, who we socialize with, how hard we will try, what music we listen to, which sports to play, what attitude we will display towards family, friends, and school and how we choose to bounce back from setbacks or adversity. As we grow older, we can choose when to leave school, and what career path to follow. The more conversations I have with teenagers about these life issues, the quicker they grasp the importance of their power to make the choices that can positively impact their lives.

A time of profound changes

Adolescence is a time of profound changes. Three of the most significant changes of the life cycle take place during this time:

1. The ability to reproduce.
2. The establishment of an identity.
3. The development of logical and rational thought processes.

---

6. Brock. *Stilling the Mind*.

CHOICES

Psychologist Jean Piaget and educator and medical doctor Maria Montessori's beliefs that a child's mind develops in fits and starts followed by periods of consolidation are being confirmed by brain development research.

Most of the conversations I have with adolescents help them to understand that choices have consequences, and how to take ownership of these choices at a time when their brain is still developing, and the prefrontal cortex (the CEO area of the brain which participates in complex decision-making) is not fully developed until their mid-twenties.

As teenagers develop their self-efficacy, they start to believe in their ability to *make* positive choices, to achieve goals and *make* change. With support from trusted adults, they take ownership—or become self-empowered, if you like—with qualities of love, gratitude, vitality, curiosity and hope, all strengths researchers believe make us happier.

Clinical psychologist Professor George W. Burns states:

> Researchers have explored what factors contribute to the happiness of the top ten per cent of happy people and the answer was very clear: the single, most important variable was that 'very happy' people had good, positive social relationships with other people. Relationships are perhaps the most important source of life satisfaction, happiness and emotional wellbeing. [7]

This is why the development of positive and meaningful relationships between adults and youth lies at the heart of the CHOICES framework.

5 SPIRIT OF MENTORING TIPS AND STRATEGIES

1. The mentoring relationship is between you and a young person, and not their parents, siblings or other family members.

---

[7]. Street and Porter. *Better than OK*, 74.

2. Meet and greet. When you meet a young person for the first time, share expectations and negotiate how this partnership will evolve.
3. Mentors drive the relationship during the early weeks. As the connection with a young person develops, the mentor allows them to steer the relationship.
4. Mentors always ask permission before they give feedback to youth.
5. Mentors are a consistent, non-judgmental cheerleader in a young person's life. The young person hears a consistent message: "Strive to become the best person *you* can be—*your* goals, *your* dreams."

CONVERSATIONS 2 CONNECT

1. What was the first thing that made you laugh today?
2. Do you have a favorite item? Jewelry? Item of clothes? Souvenir? Is this something you really value and would be shattered if it was broken or lost (not a cellphone)?
3. Describe your "ideal" teacher.
4. What are your favorite books or magazines? Why this choice? What is just one favorite book? (Or, you can ask about YouTube or video clips).
5. Imagine Aladdin arrives in your home with his magic lamp. The genie appears and grants you three wishes. What would they be?
6. Did you have a favorite toy when you were young? What happened to it?
7. You are in a shop and have paid for your purchase. You are given too much change. How do you respond?

Chapter 3

Peter's Story: Our Choices Define Us

> Your opinion of yourself begins on the inside with your character. What do you believe in, and are you willing to stand up for it despite what others may think or say? It's what my dad meant when he said, "Be true to yourself." This comes first, then the opinion of others.
>
> JOHN WOODEN[1]

A GOOD WAY TO share the CHOICES framework is by way of an illustration—a true story, a journey I became involved in, quite by chance.

Peter was about sixteen when our paths first crossed, an angry young man who felt that the world was against him. He appeared to be rebelling against anyone in a position of authority at school—I suspect also at home. I can't recall why he was in trouble, though it would have been a serious breach of the school code of

---

1. Wooden. *Wooden*, 52.

conduct if he had to spend the lunch break at the Wellbeing Centre where I had my office. Here he would have time to reflect on his behavior and the reasons he was isolated from his friends for an important part of his day.

First, a brief outline of how behavior was monitored at the school and which was linked to the red behavior monitoring card Peter received. A serious breach of the school code of conduct resulted in a red card. After two weeks all going well, Peter would progress to an orange card for a week and, finally, to a yellow card for another week. His card had to be signed at the end of every lesson by his teachers, also by his tutor and his parents. The purpose behind this process was to monitor his behavior, to look for opportunities to encourage him, and to communicate with him if any issues were still unresolved. Students understood that it was a way to guide them, with a strong focus on their health and wellbeing.

The positive aspect of the behavior monitoring card system aimed at affirming the efforts of students, and ultimately promoting the development of intrinsic motivation—behavior that is driven by internal rewards without any obvious external awards. All students arriving at the school began with a green card. As they connected with the school, contributed and became involved in a variety of ways in and out of the classroom, they progressed from green, to blue, to silver and eventually would achieve the much-treasured gold card at some point during their final eighteen months at school. However, not all students embraced the system. Peter did not embrace it.

The behavior monitoring card system was well established at the school, though we continually evaluated the behavior system, and changes occurred in the years ahead.

At this time, I was an assistant head of the school. My most important role was to oversee the pastoral care of all members of a co-educational school community of about 1400 students and staff.

I spoke to Peter's head of house—all students were allocated to a house for individual pastoral care, academic monitoring, and interhouse extracurricular competitions and activities—and was

CHOICES

informed that there had been a pattern of poor behavior and he was concerned about the choices Peter was making. There were unproven rumors that Peter was dabbling with drugs. We agreed that, in my non-disciplinary pastoral care role, I should have a chat to him.

What is going on in the brain?

Before continuing with Peter's story, let's place his behavior within the context of what neuroscience teaches us about why adolescents clash so often with adults and authority figures.

The key point is that adolescents process emotions differently from adults. They are ruled far more by their emotions than by reasoning and logic. They experience emotions before they can verbally articulate them. Therefore, it is fairly obvious that more of their thinking and decision-making takes place in the emotional parts of their brain, particularly the small almond-shaped area known as the amygdala—"a sort of anger"[2] which can lead to emotional outbursts as, for example, when an adolescent does not have their way. And, when the amygdala is overactive, they are unable to connect to others when in a state of fear or distrust. This was probably the space Peter was in when we met for the first time.

We can understand, therefore, how youth misread social situations and emotional signals from others. They often find it difficult to see and appreciate the consequences of their actions and decisions.

And, as we read in the previous chapter, the last part of the adolescent brain to fully mature is the prefrontal cortex, the area of the brain in which more rational, higher-level cognitive functioning takes place.

---

2. Jensen. *The Teenage Brain*.

Peter's Story: Our Choices Define Us

Connecting with Peter

During a lunch break I called Peter into my office and asked if he was comfortable for me to have a chat with him. I reassured him that I was in a non-disciplinary role and was looking for ways to encourage and support him. Peter agreed to talk and gave me permission to take notes, despite the folded arms and expression of anger through his body language.

I was amazed at how honest he was in our first meeting. In a nutshell, he felt disconnected from the school, was disengaged, allowed negative peer pressure to impact his behavior, felt he was drifting aimlessly through life and wasn't too concerned about that, had experimented with drugs, and was doing no exercise. Peter felt he was doing enough academically to keep people off his back. He admitted that he was anti *anyone* in authority, though couldn't really explain those feelings. Peter was strong-willed, an independent thinker with a part-time job (eleven hours a week), and had an interest in playing the saxophone.

So began our journey. I quickly saw that my role would be to guide Peter along a pathway of his choice. *Choice* became the key word, as I wanted him to take ownership of the choices he made, and the consequences that flowed from those choices.

I shared some neuroscience research with him which linked to his behavior. This led to a deeper, more positive conversation. Clearly, I was talking with an intellectually above-average student. He was also genuinely interested in brain research, particularly with regard to how it was relevant to his adolescent journey, a topic we often spoke about in the months ahead.

I asked Peter what career he would choose to follow if he had to leave school that day, had all the qualifications he required, yet had to pay rental, travel, food and clothing expenses. His interest was either to become a lawyer or a paramedic because he wished to follow a pathway that helped others—a fascinating insight.

Our conversation led to an exploration of tertiary study options. My aim was to encourage Peter to chase *his* dream, one which he was unlikely to attain without re-engaging with the school.

CHOICES

Think outside the box—Peter feels cared for

My first major challenge, though, was to arrive at the end of the term, at which point Peter would have finished the completion of the yellow card so he could start a new term with a clean slate. Some short-cuts were needed to attain this. The negotiations began. Once Peter saw that I was trying to help him, and that I cared about his future, his attitude began to change in a variety of positive ways.

A colleague informed me that, when Peter was in the junior school, he had been part of a team of students who organized an interhouse touch football competition. An idea was birthed.

I suggested to Peter that, if he chose to give something back to the community, we could have him off all cards by the end of term. He agreed to this and, when I suggested that, together with a couple of friends, he organize the junior school interhouse touch football tournament to be held during the final week of the term, he asked if he could have a couple of days to think about this.

A couple of days later he accepted the offer. The fact that he wanted time to reflect before responding was a positive step in itself, as Peter was weighing up the consequences of any choice he made. The self-empowering journey was under way.

Instead of being isolated during the lunch breaks, he visited the junior school to discuss the composition of the tournament, spoke to the students with regard to the draw of matches for the tournament, explained the tournament rules, and organized for two of his peers to referee the matches.

A junior school teacher worked alongside Peter and the students—another significant and positive adult quietly entered Peter's life.

Needless to say, the tournament went well. Although Peter didn't look too comfortable as the organizer of the tournament, he did a great job. I sent him a copy of a photo of himself handing over the tournament trophy to the captains of the winning house, and suggested he keep it somewhere safe so he could share a story of his life with others at an appropriate time.

Peter's Story: Our Choices Define Us

Peter's life gains meaning and purpose

While Peter organized the tournament, we met to discuss what he needed to do if he wanted to follow his chosen career path. Naturally this led to a discussion about setting personal specific, measurable, and realistic academic goals, writing them down, and then chasing them. Once he did this, he was on his way. My role was to speak to the potential he seemed unable to see at the time.

My initial focus was on his academic studies. Peter's goals resulted in him gradually reconnecting with the school. I looked for every opportunity to name his strengths, and use them as foundation stones for the way forward, an evidence-based approach to develop resiliency.

Peter was adamant that he would not play any sport that year, but would think about participating during his final year. We spoke about the need to have eight or nine hours sleep each night and how important that was for his brain development, as well as living a well-balanced lifestyle, which included paying attention to his diet. Fortunately, he could see the value of such a lifestyle and did not take long to move into a positive space in these areas.

Peter feels valued

Peter continued with saxophone lessons outside of school hours, which kept him involved in something in the extra-curricular that was mostly an interest or hobby. He openly expressed his disappointment when he did not pass his grade eight saxophone practical exam.

I asked him what had happened and, without hesitation, he stated, "I didn't practice enough." While he did not continue with saxophone lessons and declined to participate in any of the school music bands, a different opportunity arose when the school decided to perform a new musical, written by a highly-talented past student. This musical was promoted as a world premiere of classics from some well-known movies.

The head of music, aware of Peter's abilities, was keen to have him audition for the musical. Peter and I met to discuss this unique opportunity. I reassured him that, as he was in his final year of school with many academic pressures, he would not have to participate in any other music program at the school if he was selected for the musical band. What an opportunity to showcase his ability and take a wonderful memory with him when he left school.

Peter took a while to buy into the idea. He just beat the audition deadline. There were no other saxophone players of his standard so, shortly before the end of his penultimate year at school, Peter participated in the early musical band rehearsals.

By the end of that same year, Peter was close to achieving academic results more reflective of his undoubted potential. I sensed that his life had more meaning and purpose, he felt valued, and seemed committed to finishing his final school year well.

Finish well

True to his word, Peter became a student role-model (most of the time) during his final year at school. He participated in a summer and a winter team sport, and was one of the house senior students who led the traditional cheer leading—with his saxophone—at interhouse carnivals. I watched as many of these activities as I could, an opportunity to chat and affirm his efforts for a couple of minutes perhaps after a match or an event.

A significant highlight was the standing ovation the cast and band received at the end of each performance of the musical.

Peter passed his final year academic subjects comfortably, though possibly didn't push himself as much as he might have had he been more intrinsically motivated. He told me that he felt he was working hard enough to achieve results that would allow him to progress to the tertiary course of his choice, and that was all that was important to him. He still had to fully grasp the challenge of setting personal best goals and striving to achieve them.

Peter's Story: Our Choices Define Us

Rather than go straight to university after school, Peter took a year off and travelled overseas, using his savings from his part-time job which had also enabled him to buy a second-hand car during his final year of school (another goal achieved).

About ten months after he had left school, I was walking in the school grounds and heard someone call my name. Cheerful, polite, with positive body language, Peter shook my hand, shared some of his travel experiences, and told me that he hoped to enter university the following year to pursue a career as a paramedic.

This young man with a compassionate and caring heart, an above-average intellect, and with other abilities in music and sport, will do well in life, of that I have little doubt.

Building a meaningful relationship with Peter—reflections

I often reflect on my journey with Peter and try to pinpoint exactly what it was that led to the changing heart and attitude. Maybe it was because he felt someone who cared for him listened, valued, and respected his opinions, spoke into the potential he was hesitant to see, sat with him and allowed him to set *his* goals, and then quietly encouraged him in the background as he came to see that his life had significant meaning and purpose. Maybe I connected with him, as I had experienced a time of being a non-conformist and loner at a similar age.

Instead of Peter hearing a message like, "You go and do it!", he heard, "*Let's* go and do this! *Let's* make this happen."

Perhaps my experience with Peter supports psychologist Andrew Fuller's belief that "most teenagers only remember three things from most conversations.

1. That they are a good person who has the power to change things.
2. That talking to me was helpful.

3. That I am someone who has hope that they can find a way to have a happier life."[3]

Or, perhaps it also echoes the thoughts of psychologist Dr. Sue Roffey:

> Using strength-based language and helping kids become the people they want to be—holding high expectations that are achieved in small steps—will seed a child who is likely to grow into their own person: complete, confident, self-assured, empathic, connected and able to love life and engage with all it has to offer.[4]

When we first met, Peter feared chasing a dream in case he failed, and so he chose a negative pathway of antisocial behavior. During our time together he learnt that it was okay to step out of his comfort zone, risk failure, indeed even fail, yet to reflect on the experience and take new learning experiences into the next phase of his life. In a way Peter's journey was strange, as I could see that, whenever he wanted to do so, he could stand apart from his peers and be his own person. He had that resilient strength of character and the courage to be true to himself through the choices he made.

Embrace the CHOICES framework

Peter's story is a great example of how, over an eighteen-month period, he embraced the CHOICES framework. He developed some important foundations for his lifelong journey and became a more resilient young man with developing interests. He understood the meaning of following a healthy lifestyle, which included eight or nine hours sleep each night; how to chase his own realistic, achievable goals; how to plan and organize his time effectively; how to actively pursue an interest or a hobby; the importance of regular exercise; appreciating the importance of interdependence in his personal growth, and giving of himself to others without expecting anything in return. Possibly a key discovery was the importance of

3. Street and Porter. *Better than OK*, 135.
4. Street and Porter. *Better than OK*, 125.

trusting others—especially adults who clearly believed in him—to guide him on the journey to fulfil his potential.

Peter learnt how he had the opportunity to determine the future development of his brain through the activities and experiences in which he chose to engage—something neuroscience research continues to confirm.

Francis Jensen[5] explains best what might have occurred during my time with Peter. She wrote of the findings of a survey carried out by the National Institute of Health [in recent years] to examine how the brain regions activate one another during the first twenty-one years of life. The survey found that the connectivity of the brain slowly moves from the back of the brain to the front. The last places to "connect" are the frontal lobes.

The survey discovered that the teenage brain is 80 per cent of the way to maturity. The 20 per cent gap, where the wiring is thinnest, is crucial. This gap helps us understand the inconsistent, often impulsive behavior of teenagers like Peter—mood swings, explosiveness, irritability, an inability to focus for any length of time, or to follow through and connect with adults; their temptations to use drugs, alcohol, and to engage in other risky and antisocial behaviors.

Jensen highlights the importance, therefore, of continually talking to youth about what responsible choices feel like, look like, and sound like, as the brain is finally formed and connected in their mid-twenties. Peter and I certainly had many discussions about his choices and the meaning of accountability for those choices.

Peter's journey also supports Daniel Siegel's teaching. He describes adolescence as "an essential time of emotional intensity, social engagement and creativity . . . a period of life [which] is in reality the one with the most power for courage and creativity." Peter's choices give credibility to Siegel's belief that "how we navigate the adolescent years has a direct impact on how well we'll live the rest of our lives."[6]

5. Jensen. *The Teenage Brain.*
6. Siegel. *Brainstorm,* 6.

Knowledge is constructed

A key theme in adolescent development literature is that knowledge is constructed. We build our brains through our learning experiences, as occurred during Peter's final eighteen months at school. The nature of the learning experiences we undertake dictate how the brain develops and the connections that are pruned. Youth can develop four key life skills—the ability to

1. Reflect on learning.
2. Link new knowledge to existing knowledge.
3. Establish what is true and accurate.
4. Challenge what knowledge is untrue and inaccurate.

Knowledge that is delivered in a variety of contexts and through a range of learning strategies is more likely to be applied or transferred broadly. Organizing information and making explicit links between concepts—the spirit of mentoring in action—help youth to store and apply this knowledge. As youth specialize, they need to have an in-depth grasp of the relationships between concepts and the way knowledge is organized within a discipline, as well as factual information related to the subject.

Youth like to learn when activities are made emotionally relevant to them. Use their hobbies and interests, or a favorite TV program to spark positive emotions, which promotes their learning—strategies Peter and I discussed during our time together.

Peter's self-learning and self-empowering journey launched him on a new, positive pathway best described by leadership expert John Townsend: "People with good character are able to extend their hearts and reach other people's hearts and let other people into their hearts."[7]

---

7. Barna. *Master Leaders*.

Peter's Story: Our Choices Define Us

Developing great relationships with youth

My adolescent journey experiences and Peter's story give practical meaning and credibility to the Search Institute's *Developmental Relationship Framework* which goes hand-in-glove with the CHOICES framework:

1. Express care. "Show me that I matter to you."
2. Challenge growth. "Push me to keep getting better."
3. Provide support. "Help me to complete tasks and achieve goals."
4. Share power. "Treat me with respect and allow me to have a say."
5. Expand possibilities. "Connect me with people and places that broaden my world."[8]

In the chapters that follow, we'll consider each of the key elements of the CHOICES framework which, when taken together, are a proven framework to guide youth to achieve greatness, or to reach their potential.

First, we need to develop the key meaningful relationship for deeper conversations to occur. These relationships often progress in response to a question I often ask when meeting someone for the first time, "How can I help you?"

Some teenagers might choose not to participate, or do not believe that they have to change their ways, their decision often impacted by peer pressure, family expectations, or other challenging issues they face. Where this is the case—and there have been many such occasions in my interactions with youth—I become a seed sower who sowed CHOICE "possibility" seeds that might sprout one day when that teenager is ready. It does happen and that is why I choose never to quit on a young person.

---

8. Search Institute. *Developmental Relationships*.

CHOICES

5 SPIRIT OF MENTORING TIPS AND STRATEGIES

1. Coach youth how to appreciate that *their* choices will define how *they* move forward in life. Always share thoughts as you help them understand that every choice has a consequence.
2. Most youth enjoy discussing the adolescent brain. This is also a topic you can research together.
3. Effective mentors never stop learning—they are teachable. This is an important quality to share with youth.
4. Mentors are selfless—the focus is *always* on the young person, their needs, and wishes. Continually remind them that success is about achieving *their* unique potential, and *never* about comparing themselves to others.
5. Mentors have a great sense of humor. They coach youth how to laugh at themselves, and not to take life too seriously.

CONVERSATIONS 2 CONNECT

1. Are you familiar with the term "bucket list"—things you would like to do in your lifetime? What would be the top six items on your bucket list if you wrote one today?
2. What do you think are the arguments for and against students having to wear a school uniform? (in situations where this topic is relevant)
3. There is an opinion that students should not have to do homework. What are your thoughts?
4. There is a suggestion that violent video games make people more violent? What are your thoughts? What video games do you enjoy, and how do they affect you?
5. Describe your perfect day to me.
6. What one little thing really bugs, or annoys, or irritates you? Why?

7. Imagine you are alone in a deserted area. Someone from outer space arrives who can speak your language. You are not frightened. What would you talk about?

Chapter 4

Clear Goals

If you want to be happy set a goal that commands your thoughts, liberates your energy and inspires your hopes.

ANDREW CARNEGIE

THE STRENGTH OF THE CHOICES framework is its flexibility. It can be adapted to an individual's circumstances. All the key elements are interlinked to provide skills for a positive lifelong journey.
Psychologist David Walsh states that

> ... the brain develops in fits and starts ... every brain function seems to have its own timetable and, as the young person grows and responds to the challenges of the environment in which they are living, different parts of the brain become more active than other parts. Neuroscience research now can inform us that the brain actually remains quite malleable in cognitive and emotional development during adolescence and even into adulthood. This is encouraging for anyone working with young people as it contains a message of hope that, no

matter how awful the circumstances might be, there *is* a positive pathway that can be chosen.[1]

This knowledge reinforces the value of the CHOICES framework, as it encourages anyone guiding adolescents to appreciate that they are involved in a process of experimenting with solutions to assist a young person find the best way forward for themselves. The non-negotiable point, though, is never to encourage anything that can be remotely life-threatening.

So, as I mentor a young person, they embark on a journey aimed at figuring out for themselves what works and what doesn't work. During this journey, I am the non-judgmental cheerleader who encourages them to identify their passion and chase their dreams. I discover their passion through conversation, and then begin the process of encouraging them to think about setting some realistic and achievable goals. As they strive to achieve their goals, they learn more about themselves.

This, therefore, is a good time to introduce the first key element of the CHOICES framework: *Clear Goals*.

Why set goals?

Mentoring expert Dr. Susan Weinberger highlights five reasons why youth should set goals. It is a chance to

1. Choose where they want to go.
2. Decide what they want to achieve.
3. Know where to concentrate their efforts.
4. Spot the distractions that would lure them from their course.
5. Build self-confidence which grows faster when they set and achieve goals.[2]

---

1. Walsh. *Why do they?*
2. Weinberger. *Correspondence.*

CHOICES

Girls' and Boys' brains

Not too long ago, adolescence was described as beginning around the age of thirteen and ending around the age of seventeen. That is no longer the case. Adolescence can now last at least fifteen years, which is why creating a goal setting plan can be such a powerful skillset for lifelong learning.

Girls enter puberty at about ten or eleven years of age and, on average, have completed their growth spurt by the age of sixteen. Boys tend to enter puberty when they are twelve or thirteen and their growth spurt continues until they are about eighteen. Throughout the awkwardness of adolescence, girls are about two years ahead of the game.

Some research indicates that male brains are on average between ten and fifteen per cent larger than female brains, though a bigger brain does *not* indicate more brain power.

For boys the main growth hormone is testosterone which triggers the major physical changes, like dramatic growth spurts and sudden voice changes. Adolescent boys can have between five and ten surges of testosterone every day during the course of puberty. By the end of adolescence, they can have 1000 per cent the amount of testosterone in their bodies than they had before puberty, and fifteen to twenty times more than girls have at the same age.

Testosterone affects both the body and the brain. Specifically, testosterone has a powerful effect on the amygdala—the part of the brain protecting us from harm, which activates the "fight or flight" reflex. The amygdala has receptors for testosterone, so in the midst of puberty, especially during a hormonal surge, the amygdala is regularly overstimulated. As a result, boys become emotional powder kegs. While testosterone does all sorts of good things, it is also likely to trigger surges of anger, aggression, sexual interest, dominance and territoriality. And because testosterone is geared toward quick tension release, adolescent boys are prone to follow any impulse that might release stress.

Clear Goals

For girls, the two important growth hormones are estrogen (which is actually a family of different hormones) and progesterone. Estrogen triggers the physical changes in girls: the development of breasts, widening of the pelvis, the onset of menstruation and all the other physical changes. Estrogen affects the brain as well.

Whereas the amygdala has a lot of docking stations for testosterone, it's the hippocampus—the memory centre—where estrogen molecules find an abundance of welcoming ports. This connection may give girls some advantage when it comes to academic tasks requiring memory. Girls have about ten times more estrogen than boys.

Skill development

Girls' brains seem to be equipped to acquire language skills faster than boys' brains, but that doesn't mean an individual boy will be unable to learn languages quickly if his experiences support such learning. According to educator Sheryl Feinstein[3], girls, in general, tend to have better verbal skills, boys better spatial awareness, and both sexes are capable of learning and remembering as much and as thoroughly.

The simple explanation for the jump that girls' brains have developmentally on boys, as already mentioned, is that they reach puberty earlier. The gradual shift of emotional processing from the amygdala to the prefrontal cortex happens earlier for girls than it does for boys. At the end of adolescence most boys' brains have caught up to girls' brain development.

The teenager's brain development improves through *effort*—the more we try and make our brain behave the way we want it to be, the quicker it will do so.

Expressed another way, author and brain researcher Nicola Morgan explains:

---

3. Feinstein. *Secrets.*

> ... the brain operates in a "use it or lose it" basis ... it develops networks because you try something, do something, practice something. The more you do, and the more different activities you take part in, the better your brain will be at those activities and the better it will work in general, because a good brain is one where all the parts work well together."[4]

If youth are guided to develop a positive view of the future, they can be happy and appreciate that their lives have meaning and purpose, and experience a growth mindset.

Develop an effective goal setting strategy

An effective goal setting strategy assists positive brain development, and involves an exciting journey of self-learning and self-discovery. Space does not allow us to go into great depth about goal setting. Three of my books, *The Spirit of Mentoring: a manual for volunteer adults*, *The Mentoring Spirit of the Teacher*, and *Letter 2 a Teen—Becoming the Best I can Be,* contain detailed sections dedicated to the importance of setting specific, measurable, intentional, limited, extending and realistic goals. I call these SMILER goals, the idea being to see goal setting, then goal getting, as fun rather than a chore or something a young person has to do because an adult tells them to set goals.

Therein lies the key point about a clear goal setting plan: the goals *must* be decided by the adolescent and linked to *their* personal vision of what their future might look like. These become "personal best" goals, which tend to be developed most effectively with a significant adult when trust and mutual respect has been established.

---

4. Morgan. *Blame My Brain*, 180.

The goal setting process

How do we encourage young people to think realistically about the future?

As I shared in Peter's story in the previous chapter, an easy way to encourage discussion is simply to ask a teenager what they would do for a job if they had to leave school today. They have to pay for food, clothes, rent, transport, and other daily necessities. This would mean they have to find a job. However, they have all the qualifications they need. What job would they choose?

Responses to such questioning create fascinating discussions. The focus is on the teenager, not their parents' ambitions for them, and thus the self-empowerment journey begins to take shape.

Inevitably this discussion can lead to a look at possible tertiary level studies, subjects to study at school, or requirements a specific job or interest demands. Suddenly the light goes on in the life of this teenager as they discover some meaning and purpose for their lives. It is also important to continually stress to the young person that this journey involves striving to achieve *their* personal best goals. It has nothing to do with competing against others, as Rachel discovered.

Rachel's story

Rachel was in continuous trouble during her final year of school. She had an explosive personality and her peers knew how to wind her up. Her academic results were woefully inconsistent and there was a real chance that she would leave school with little to show for her time there unless she changed her attitude.

The process I followed with Rachel was similar to that which I followed with Peter. We chatted about her dreams and goals. At that point, she acknowledged she would achieve little because she was falling behind with her work and not meeting important deadlines. My role was to paint a picture of hope for her, encourage her to buy into it, support her on the journey, and make sure that she finished her schooling well.

CHOICES

Rachel identified that her real passion in life was to enter the nursing profession, preferably to become a midwife. When we explored the academic requirements for university, it was clear that, without a considerable change of attitude, greater planning and organization, together with more self-discipline, it would be almost impossible to fulfil her nursing dream. Indeed, aware of her poor academic results, Rachel had a defeatist attitude. She did not believe she could, in the time available, produce the academic results to study nursing. I challenged her to prove herself wrong, and stressed to her that, with a more disciplined approach, her dream was attainable.

We worked on her goals and initially placed a special focus on her academic goals and key aspects of her planning and organization (management of time). For example, we drew up timelines to make sure assignments were completed ahead of time, rather than by the deadline. In this way Rachel understood that she would have some extra time available in case something cropped up that impacted her schedule.

Rachel took a few months to develop a workable organization and planning process. I was okay with this, as I kept reminding her that she was also developing life skills which would help her beyond school. There was trial and error, some admitted laziness, some half-hearted efforts in a couple of subjects she did not enjoy, and it took her a while to appreciate that there were no short cuts to achieving her goals—a consistent effort was required within a healthy and balanced lifestyle. I remained the consistent voice with a clear message: "You can do this. I believe in you."

I shared ideas about how she could achieve her dream, though stressed that I could not do the work for her. We also discussed how to develop positive relationships with a variety of friendship groups—which included greater self-control—and how to positively resolve conflicts.

The goal setting experience proved to be one of the many turning points in Rachel's journey. She embraced the goals, improved her effort, and finally was able to study nursing at university. Rachel is now a qualified nurse and loving her career.

Rachel learnt that she actually had control of her future and her destiny. She had control of her thoughts. When she focused on more positive self-talk, and had the courage to do what she initially seemed afraid to do, she began to see positive change occur. She learnt how to turn problems and challenges into new opportunities for personal growth. She also became teachable and coachable.

How to set meaningful goals

Having identified a career pathway, we have an open and honest discussion with a focus on recent academic results, relevance of school or study, and making the most of opportunities. I write the key points down, in this case with Rachel's permission, and then ask the young person to estimate their results if they work consistently hard for their next exams.

My role is to challenge *their* reality. For example, if the student is failing three out of six subjects, it's unrealistic to set high goals for each subject, given the self-discipline that needs to be applied to academic studies, or possibly having to catch up work missed or not completed. However, if I discern that the student is capable of achieving outstanding results with some consistent effort the goals will reflect this.

John Wooden offers a helpful thought: "Mix idealism with realism and add hard work. This will often bring much more than you could ever hope for."[5]

Then we break this process down into bite-sized, doable chunks, or small action plans. After the exams or tests, we'll compare the results achieved against the goals set, and then revisit the goals. I keep a copy of the goals and the teenager with whom I work also keeps a copy of their goals which they have written down and are now accountable for.

My experience is that, once youth start to see the results of their efforts, they embrace the goal setting process, and their lives take on significance. They develop more positive characteristics

---

5. Wooden. *Wooden*, 64.

and competencies, explore other interests and, most important of all, their self-efficacy—their belief in their own ability to achieve things and make positive changes themselves—increases.

Three key goal setting points

We'll expand on all of this as we look at the other steps in the CHOICES framework. However, there are three important points to highlight about the goal setting journey and which can significantly impact the experience for the young person.

Firstly, it's vitally important that youth know it is okay to fail. They need to make and learn from their mistakes and grow socially, emotionally, and intellectually. Making mistakes is one key way the brain learns. Psychologist and educator Abigail James[6] reiterates the point that boys, in particular, need to understand that failing is not a blot on their masculinity; giving up is real failure. Again, the importance of having the non-judgmental adult cheerleader as the wise guide on the side to encourage the young person to chase their dreams and goals can be critical to the success or otherwise of the goal setting journey. Remember, therefore, the importance of allowing flexibility when a teenager hits a major obstacle or setback.

Although the teenage brain's learning is at peak efficiency, much else is inefficient. This includes their attention span, self-discipline, task completion, and emotions. It was important that I did not overwhelm Rachel with instructions, for example, and that she focused on completing one task at a time as she developed her self-confidence. I also reminded myself that because Rachel's brain was not yet wired to consider "distant consequences"—or, what might happen in the long-term—I had to continually explain, clarify, and paint different scenarios so she could reflect on the consequences of her choices.

---

6. James. *Teaching*.

Clear Goals

Daniel Siegel stresses that, "For both adolescent and adult, keeping the lines of communication open is the most basic principle of navigating these [adolescent] years well."[7]

Some students take longer than others to embrace the goal setting process. I always begin by encouraging the student to set a fairly straightforward goal that they know they can achieve with a minimum effort. It is the *process* I want them to take ownership of and, as they do so, their feelings change, their level of self-belief rises, and we reach a point where they are ready to move out of their comfort zone and reach for the stars.

Secondly, an area that is often overlooked by significant adults is when and how to give feedback. Youth don't just want feedback they actually *crave* it as it helps them complete their learning. They appreciate quick feedback while the task or assignment, for example, remains fresh in their minds. Feedback improves the brain's efficiency. Most important, without information about their performance, the teenager's brain won't know what neurons to grow or which ones to prune.

Sheryl Feinstein[8] describes how positive feedback actually releases serotonin into the brain, a chemical that reinforces feelings of calm and happiness. She states that feedback in the classroom and in life is one of the most important ways we can help youth turn their brains into efficient learning systems.

Remember, when you give feedback, look for *performance* not perfection. Let the young person respond to a question like, "How do I rate compared to what I see myself becoming?"

I always ask youth for permission to give them feedback, because they need to be in the right frame of mind when such a discussion occurs. And, when I give feedback in a positive and constructive way, within an environment of trust, there is a better than even chance that the young person will benefit positively from the discussion.

The third crucially important point about the goal setting journey is to make sure that it remains a fun experience. A sense

---

7. Siegel. *Brainstorm*, 26.
8. Feinstein. *Secrets*.

of humor is vital. Remember, teenagers are processing emotions differently from adults; they often misread situations and emotional signals from others; they are on a tumultuous and confusing journey as they discover who they are, where they are going, and with whom. Not only do they need to learn to laugh at themselves, but they also need to be reminded to retain a sense of humor. We know, from research, that the average young person has a great sense of humor, so this should not be a difficult button to press within a trusting environment.

Rachel and I enjoyed a fun relationship as we both possessed a great sense of humor and could laugh at ourselves.

Times of self-doubt

While there are inevitably a variety of challenges teenagers face when they embark on the goal setting journey, such as the fear of failure, lack of self-belief, procrastination, laziness, negative peer pressure, and a reluctance to move out of their comfort zone, most young people respond positively to encouragement from a trusted adult cheerleader.

When a young person questions the value of setting goals, remind them that some of the key results of goal setting from years of research include: having a sense of meaning and purpose; having a focus; being able to achieve more with our lives; helping eliminate negative attitudes; improving management of time skills; reducing stress and anxiety; improving concentration, and teaching us how to deal with setbacks; developing resiliency; improving performance, and boosting our self-confidence.

Remember to start the process with easy to achieve goals, as that builds the early confidence. Then start stretching, expanding out of the comfort zone, and at all times make sure that the goals are specific, realistic and measurable. And goals must *always* be the young person's *personal* goals—never those of a parent, teacher, or another significant adult—as the meaningful change begins in the *heart*.

Make sure, too, that the goals are *written* down by the student, and also encourage them to visualize themself actually *achieving* the goals—these two skills are effective and meaningful methods of self-empowerment. When they learn how to visualize their goals, you encourage an ability to analyze important thought processes—critical thinking—for the world of work: imagination, creativity, and innovation.

It is also worthwhile for the young person to write down a statement—which they can refer to regularly—written in the present tense, as if they have achieved the goal already. This gives them a sense of ownership. So, for example, Peter might have written, "I am driving home in my new car [Make and Model], the result of all my savings from my part-time work. I feel chuffed!" Rachel might write down: "I am pinching myself as I arrive for my first day at University. Awesome feeling to think that I'll be nursing soon."

Summary

Finally, reflect on some of psychologist Professor Andrew Martin's research with regard to setting personal best goals. He found that personal best goals are associated with "positive education aspirations; enjoyment of school; class participation and persistence . . . as well as . . . deep learning, academic flow and positive relationships with teachers." He states that personal best goals have led to "literacy and numeracy achievement, test effort and homework completion."[9]

Through this goal setting process, therefore, we promote the growth mindset mentioned in an earlier chapter, as youth come to appreciate that their competence and skills can be developed through effort and a positive attitude, and that they have the room and the potential to grow academically. Coach them how to see the word "failure" as a negative swear word they can erase from their vocabulary. There might be temporary setbacks which cause

---

9. Street and Porter. *Better than OK,* 21.

them to pause, reflect, learn, and then push on towards the goal. A setback becomes the starting-point for the next effort.

Be encouraged by the findings of psychologist Richard Guare and educator, Peg Dawson: "Neuroscience research tells us that the adolescent brain is primed for the acquisition of new skills. Teens are driven to seek out new experiences, more intense social and emotional relationships and, for better or worse, new risks."[10]

So, remind them not only to goal set, but also to "goal get" and, as they take that step from the known into the unknown, growth occurs.

5 SPIRIT OF MENTORING TIPS AND STRATEGIES

1. Mentors seek to connect with youth—this requires empathy and discussions to discern the young person's hobbies, interests, dreams and possible career goals. Mentors use questions like: "How can I help you?" "How can I make this [situation] better? Is there any way I can add some value to . . . ?"

2. Mentors always make sure that youth set their own personal best goals— "These are *your* goals." During the early stages of the relationship—especially when the young person is not a goal setter—keep the goals simple, realistic, measurable, and achievable with a short time-frame, and build from there.

3. Mentors always focus on a young person's *efforts*, rather than performance. They want youth to become the heroes of their own stories.

4. Mentors celebrate the small victories with youth as *each* goal is achieved.

5. Mentors coach youth how to stretch themselves, step outside their comfort zone, and never to accept a second-rate or half-hearted effort as they strive to reach *their* potential.

---

10. Guare and Dawson. *Smart*, 3.

CONVERSATIONS 2 CONNECT

1. What was a gift that you received from someone that really meant a lot to you?
2. What are your favorite movies? Violence? Travel? Adventure? Comedy? Romance? Science Fiction? Is there one favorite movie you have watched a number of times?
3. Tell me about the most interesting person you have met to date? Why was that person so interesting?
4. If you were given the opportunity to spend four weeks wherever you liked, all expenses paid, where would you go?
5. Imagine you only have two years left on earth. What would you want to achieve by the end of that time, so that people will appreciate the difference you have tried to make?
6. What does the word "success" mean to you? Or, what would "success" look like for you? (Have the discussion and leave the young person with a copy of John Wooden's definition of "success" as an example: "Success is peace of mind, which is a direct result of self-satisfaction in knowing you made the effort to become the best of which you are capable." (John Wooden))
7. Who was your hero when you were growing up? Or, who is your hero today? What made that person, or those people special?

Chapter 5

Hobbies and Interests

> Live your life from your heart. Share from your heart. And your story will touch and heal people's souls.
>
> MELODY BEATTIE

THE PREVIOUS CHAPTER FOCUSED on the importance of having clear goals, a critical phase in the development of self-learning and self-empowerment. Indeed, effective goals give the young person a sense of pride and self-worth, with a focus on topics of interest. They develop feelings of greater independence as they learn how to make sound choices. Youth also develop an ability to respond to failures constructively and positively. They become more resilient, and they have a greater tolerance for risk-taking at a non-life-threatening level.

Daniel Siegel reminds us that "changes that occur in the adolescent brain are vitally important developmental changes that enable certain new abilities to emerge,"[1] and that's one of the reasons we keep talking about the development of the *whole* child.

---

1. Siegel. *Brainstorm*, 74.

Hobbies and Interests

The second key element within the CHOICES framework is, therefore, about pursuing *Hobbies and Interests* away from school academic pursuits.

Positive brain development

Let's link this briefly to more neuroscience research. I am leaning on some great work on the adolescent brain by JoAnn and Terrence Deak[2]. Basically, brain structures, which don't develop at the same time or at the same rate, are made up of neurons, which are the primary functional cells of the brain. We are born with approximately one hundred billion neurons, most of which we never need. As we get older, neurons become more robust and are bigger, longer and wider until they reach their full size. When the neurons are fully mature, the glial cells in the central nervous system, which support, protect and nourish neurons, remove the debris and make a fatty, waxy substance called myelin. Myelin wraps around the long axons, a long branch extending from the cell body and carrying electrical signals to the distant parts of our body. Myelin also protects these signals from breaking up as they travel. Different brain structures achieve their fully myelinated state at different ages, and as myelination becomes more extensive, the brain becomes more capable of complex skills.

Nicola Morgan[3] described how some of our neurons, called mirror neurons, fire up when we watch someone else perform an action. These same mirror neurons are used when we perform the action ourselves. So, we watch someone do something a few times. When we come to do it ourselves, it may be easier because some of our neurons have already practiced the action.

Francis Jensen explains:

> The more a piece of information is repeated or relearned, the stronger the neurons become, and the connection becomes like a well-worn path through the woods

---

2. Deak. *The Owner's*.
3. Morgan. *Blame My Brain*, 13.

CHOICES

> ... 'Frequency' and 'recency' are key words ... the more frequently and the more recently we learn something and then recall it or use it again, the more entrenched the knowledge—whether it's remembering the route between home and [school], or how to add a contact to your smart phone's directory.[4]

As adolescents take on more complex challenges in and out of the classroom, remind them that training their brain requires patience. We don't get it right immediately and need to try, try, and try again. The brain requires practice as skills are nurtured and systematically developed over time, and persistence—don't give up.

The good news is that our brains continue to give birth to new neurons *throughout* our lives, a process called neurogenesis. This happens mostly in the brain structures that are important for plasticity or learning.

Why is all this important in this chapter?

A time of exploration

During puberty our bodies are transformed by hormonal and chemical changes, and these changes often affect our interactions with others and the world around us. In addition, as we have already seen in earlier chapters, this is when we seek to become more independent. We begin to explore new interests and activities, perhaps even become more aware of global issues—"is there something I can do to put an end to global poverty?", a question I was probably not asking myself as an eight or nine-year-old. Or, "I have an idea to change ... How do I set up a small business? Who can help me?"

Youth experience new thoughts, feelings and relationships made even more complex when the intensity of romantic feelings surface. This is a natural result of the changes taking place in the

---

4. Jensen. *The Teenage Brain*.

brain as the body prepares for adult social interactions and relationships and, ultimately, reproduction.

Psychologist David Walsh describes adolescents during these times, as young people navigating a "cerebral hurricane without a compass".[5] This becomes apparent as we witness unpredictable mood swings, expressions of invincibility, and behavior that seems uncharacteristic.

Author and educator, Maggie Dent, encourages the significant adults in a teenager's life to be a "lighthouse" in their lives. "A lighthouse is something strong, reliable, immovable which shines a light showing safe passage. It does not tell you what to do, it simply shows you a safer way to go. A lighthouse doesn't rescue. It helps a young person discover the power of choices, which is what autonomy, the desire to be independent is all about.... Lighthouses are able to develop relationships with young people in which they can sow seeds of potential and shine a light on the invisible sign that hangs around every adolescent's neck: show me I matter."[6]

Youth growth spurts last about one year. Boys grow on average 4.1 inches (10.16 centimeters), girls 3.3 inches (8.89 centimeters) during this time. Weight increases during the growth spurts, shown in muscle development of boys, while girls have more fat. It's estimated according to Nicola Morgan's research[7] that 60 per cent of teenage girls are trying to lose weight at any one time, while approximately 15 to 20 per cent of youth between the ages of thirteen and eighteen experience depression, twice as many girls as boys.

Taming the hurricane

While this hurricane is causing such confusion in the lives of often frustrated teenagers, a hobby, an interest, or a passion can hold

---

5. Walsh. *Why do they?*
6. Street and Porter. *Better than OK*, 138.
7. Morgan. *Blame My Brain*, 110.

them steady, something to give them a focus when they feel overwhelmed, and are trying to stay true to themselves.

My passion in sport during my youth, which led me to read many articles and books about sport and leadership, gave me a focus beyond the pursuit of academic results. It also caused me to lead a relatively healthy and balanced lifestyle, as I placed such an emphasis on my personal fitness.

Peter's interest in music, especially the saxophone, and his part-time job, which he enjoyed, gave him a focus when he was in an anti-school frame of mind.

Rachel loved pets, played a musical instrument, and also enjoyed her part-time job which introduced her to a variety of people of all ages and from different socio-economic backgrounds.

We can encourage youth to appreciate that these are the years to sample new experiences and move out of their comfort zones. There might be short seasons participating in an activity, but each experience becomes a healthy opportunity to engage their brains. JoAnn and Terrence Deak state that the more teenagers stimulate, challenge, and stretch their minds, the more neurotrophins their brains produce. Neurotrophins are proteins produced by glial cells that act like fertilizer for their brains, stimulating neurogenesis and increasing their brain power. This is crucial because their brains become more resilient during times of stress, more capable of handling new experiences, and more likely to see them reach their potential, or achieve greatness.

Dopamine pleasure experiences

Another chemical produced by the brain is dopamine. Francis Jensen explains: "Dopamine is a special neurotransmitter as it is both excitatory and inhibitory. It is also along with epinephrine and several others, a hormone. When dopamine acts on the adrenal glands it is acting hormonally. When it acts in the brain it is a neurotransmitter which helps motivate, drive and focus the brain as it's integral to the brain's reward circuitry."[8]

So, dopamine produces the pleasure of a deep inner satisfaction and increases motivation, curiosity, perseverance, and memory. We remember those special "Wow!" moments, for example, when we have achieved a goal after a considerable effort—that satisfied, exhausted feeling. These "Wow!" moments must be recalled when we are drifting into a negative, even self-pitying space. Dopamine is released and we begin to bounce back.

As teenagers mature, if they learn how to keep developing positive skills and activities that release dopamine, they are less likely to participate in high-risk behaviors like messing with drugs or alcohol, promiscuity, reckless driving, or over-eating.

Encourage teenagers, therefore, to explore a variety of interests and then help them develop a healthy life balance. Appreciate that these interests might be more short-term than long-term, and that's okay. Sometimes they might fire a new passion that could create a positive life-changing experience.

Over the years I have often turned to a scrapbook of newspaper cuttings, letters, notes and photographs from my final year at school. I have such wonderful memories, and all those achievements and experiences remind me that I am capable and lovable. Those special memories and experiences help me to bounce back from negative moments—the dopamine release.

Acknowledge the uniqueness of every child

Interests and hobbies will vary—it could be playing board games, or a fascination with cars or motorbikes, X-box, repairing electrical gadgets, baking or cooking, photography, designing something, solving a puzzle, gardening or participating in an environmental project, reading or writing, playing a musical instrument, dance, drama or art.

---

8. Jensen. *The Teenage Brain*.

CHOICES

My passion for sport as a teenager led me to plaster my bedroom walls with my favorite sport teams, sporting heroes and, later, even a poster with a motivational quote or two. I read plenty of books and articles about my heroes, developed my own training program, and rubbed shoulders with international and state cricketers when I watched them practice. These different ways of focusing on my interests kept me chasing my dreams and goals.

Remember, we can encourage teenagers to participate in rich multi-faceted activities, aware of the fact that developing brains need challenging and socially-engaging activities and experiences.

Experienced educator Fern Van de Pol shared these thoughts with me as she read a draft of this book:

> Your focus on hobbies is also necessary. It may appear a trivial thing to many adults, who tend to think that kids need to focus on school work, and prepare for 'useful' careers. But without passions and interests, teens are left floundering, with no idea where their strengths are. As I always said to my students, people without a passion, whatever it may be (dancing, sport, music, debating, birding, whatever) are just so boring! And this is such a problem nowadays, with device time limiting the time kids have to pursue interests. Hobbies and passions teach us about our world, our strengths and weaknesses, they provide crucial stress release, and often a means to access a caring mentor. Passions often teach crucial discipline. My music and dance teacher friends are finding their task is increasingly difficult, as kids of today want to play a Beethoven sonata, or execute a perfect dance move, without the hours and hours of practice that is required. It's a life lesson . . . [9]

We can link hobbies and interests to the goal setting journey as well, simply by encouraging the teenager to set time aside each week to pursue the interest or focus to develop a specific skill—something I always do, as occurred with Sue.

---

9. Van de Pol. *Correspondence.*

Tough times require new thinking—Sue's story

How many times, as a teenager, did you feel alone and battling the world? I remember times when I was alone and trying to puzzle what life was all about. I would be asking questions like: Why me? Why can't I be like that person? Why? Why? Why?

Sixteen-year-old Sue was battling with a serious personal issue. She was a boarder at the school on a full scholarship, as she lived in a severely disadvantaged community. One afternoon she popped in to see me in my office. I was the school principal at the time. Students knew that, if my door was open, they could come and chat.

Sue started talking in fairly general ways about school, life, her favorite subjects, and things she enjoyed doing. I listened with interest. After a while she shared that she was not looking forward to returning home during the school holidays. Her father was disabled as a result of a work accident. He had been left disabled and was confined to a wheelchair. He was abusive towards her and had a violent temper. From what Sue shared, the abuse was only verbal—still, tough for a teenager whose brain was developing and prone to emotional outbursts. We needed to think through possibilities.

Explore options and be non-judgmental

We explored the different options open to Sue. I sowed some seeds to encourage her to think outside of her comfort zone. Sue reflected and responded. One idea was for Sue to apply for a United World College scholarship. This was a scholarship that would cover her education and boarding for the final two years of her education journey. She would study for the International Baccalaureate. If successful, she would be able to approach almost any university for entrance to further study. Winning such a scholarship would reduce the time she would spend at home and that meant less time possibly being abused by her father.

CHOICES

During the following week I undertook further research on this while Sue weighed up the possibilities. She remained keen to explore this option further, so I gave her the application forms which needed to be completed and signed by a parent. I stressed to Sue that it was important her parents supported this application.

Build a web of support around youth

Sue told me that her mother was fully supportive—I never asked about her father—and the forms were duly submitted. A while later Sue heard that she had been awarded a scholarship to complete her education in another country and this she did, moving to her new school at the end of that particular year.

When Sue decided to apply for the scholarship, she knew that she had to display the qualities of a genuine all-rounder. She did well academically, though she was under-performing. She had a great singing voice and participated in school choral performances, and in the school musical production that year. She worked hard to improve her social skills, as she had a tendency to annoy her peers by occasionally making insensitive comments.

Sue experienced some challenging months. However, her life gained meaning and purpose, she felt cared for and valued, and she responded positively to the challenges facing her. I remained a quiet background supporter in those months before she headed off on a wonderful adventure.

Six Lessons for Sue to reach her potential

Looking back, what life lessons can be taken from Sue's transformational experience? How did her hobbies and interests provide her with an important focus during challenging times? How could a significant adult encourage and support her as the wise guide on the side?

1. Sue arrived at a point in her life when she needed to talk to someone she respected about her situation and express her

feelings. She had courage, and chose to be vulnerable and share something that was clearly a painful part of her life, and difficult to talk about. My role was to be empathetic, encourage her, and speak to the potential she could not fully see at the time.

2. Sue received a subsidized education as her family had little money. In the discussions we had, she saw that there were opportunities for her, though hard work and consistent effort was required to take advantage of any such opportunities. There were no short-cuts available. I was sensitive to her situation, though also had to be truthful about the challenges ahead. Sue had to face the reality of her unique situation. Together we developed a realistic goal setting process which initially covered academic and non-academic activities, and would later include ways to improve her communication with peers. We moved at Sue's pace.

3. Sue could have given up, accepted her lot in life and stayed at the school. However, when she saw the opportunity to advance, to travel, and to obtain an excellent education in another country, she moved out of her comfort zone and began to chase a new dream. Her perseverance was rewarded. I helped her envision new possibilities using her gifts and talents. Her love of music, dance and drama—her hobbies and interests—provided an outlet for her to express herself. This helped her move forward in positive ways.

4. Sue was an opinionated young woman. She learnt how to express her idealism and develop a more empathetic attitude towards her peers and family members. My role was to share ideas and thoughts about building meaningful relationships with others, listen with genuine interest and concern to Sue, and guide her through a variety of ways to positively resolve conflict.

5. Sue had a warm, beautiful smile and a wonderful sense of humor. She genuinely cared about other people, and had a deep faith. She learnt how to reach out to others in need, and she

gave of herself to support people less privileged than herself. My role was to push her to do more to develop resiliency. At the same time, we talked about management of time and living a healthy and balanced lifestyle.

6. Sue chose to change her attitude towards life, school, her family, and her peers, and reaped the rewards. My role was as a seed sower who also opened her mind and eyes to what "might" be attainable.

Sue's *defining moment* was probably having the courage to trust me with her feelings about life at home. After that first discussion, she would pop into my office, maybe once a fortnight, just to chat, or we might interact when we saw one another around the school grounds. A two minutes conversation can be life-changing for an adolescent. Sue taught me plenty and, hopefully too, our interactions gave her the confidence to step out and chase her dreams.

The message for teachers and significant adults to share with youth is the importance of sharing their feelings, dreams and ideals with an adult, or adults they trust, which Sue chose to do. There is always a risk when they do this. As they discover that the person to whom they choose to speak is non-judgmental, and doesn't want to offer advice every second minute of the conversation, they discover who to trust with their deeper issues. And, a timely conversation about pursuing hobbies and interests could lead to the development of a more meaningful relationship, as I experienced with Sue.

Develop the whole child

Encourage the development of the *whole* child. Educator John Hare wrote:

> The aim of holistic education must be to prepare students for a fulfilling and productive life in which their skills and attributes are constantly challenged, developed and applied as part of their lifelong learning. It is an

educational journey of personal discovery starting within formal education then continuing throughout life.[10]

I have tried to link the key developmental stages of adolescence with brain research, as I believe many adults are ignorant about much of this research, and have yet to grasp how profound the ability of the brain actually is to rewire and remap itself because of its plasticity.

David Walsh[11] asserted that research showed an undeniable overproduction of grey matter during adolescence. This presents teenagers with the opportunity to excel in all kinds of areas. Synapses, the small spaces at the junction between two neurons where the neurotransmitter is released, according to Walsh, spawn all over their brains. If teenagers do a lot of reading, they become better readers; if they are fond of and practice a lot of science, they will probably become scientists; students who solve problems become great problem solvers. So, Walsh concludes, this is a neurological reason to involve adolescents in responsible activities, and introduce them to all kinds of new experiences.

The danger, though, and I have seen this with some teenagers, is that they become fixated on a new interest or hobby at the expense of their academic studies, even their social groups. They need direction and guidance from a trusted adult to develop a balanced and healthy lifestyle.

5 SPIRIT OF MENTORING TIPS AND STRATEGIES

1. Mentors share their hobbies and interests with youth—young people may be interested in exploring some of these hobbies and interests with their mentors.

2. Mentors explore management of time, planning and organization, and other relevant work ethic topics with youth.

---

10. Hare. *Holistic Education.*
11. Walsh. *Why do they?*

3. Mentors rarely offer advice. Through careful questioning—effective communication techniques—youth find solutions to challenges as they strive to become the best person *they* can be.
4. Mentors appreciate that focusing on a non-academic or work-related goal might eventually lead youth to appreciate the importance of academic or work-related goals.
5. Mentors keep an open mind and are prepared to move out of their comfort zones—without taking unnecessary or life-threatening risks—to guide youth to reach *their* potential.

CONVERSATIONS 2 CONNECT

1. What is your favorite hobby (or interest)? What other hobbies have you had in the past? Would you like me to share some of my interests over the years?
2. What type of music do you enjoy listening to? Why?
3. Which clubs in or out of school do you belong to?
4. What musical instruments do you play, or have you played in the past? Is there a musical instrument you would like to play?
5. Do you have a favorite clothes shop? What was your latest purchase? How much online shopping do you do?
6. Do you have a part-time job? What's it like? How many hours each week are you working? What do you like, or not like about it? Are you saving any money? Should we discuss how to budget?
7. Do you have a favorite holiday you remember? Or, a favorite place your family visits regularly?

Chapter 6

Organization

May what you see in the mirror delight you, and what others see in you delight them. May someone love you enough to forgive your faults, be blind to your blemishes, and tell the world about your virtues.

Author Unknown

Each of the key elements in the CHOICES framework is linked to guiding youth to appreciate how *every* choice they make has a consequence. Our focus, of course, is to encourage youth to make positive choices. They have no idea how amazing or great they are. They often don't appreciate how they develop a growth mindset that can take them to exciting new places when they start to believe about *positives* and *possibilities*.

The third key element within the CHOICE framework is *Organization*.

This is the area where most teenagers genuinely struggle. Ask them if they are managing their time effectively and have everything planned, and many will answer, "Yes, I've got everything organized. No, I don't need any help, as we have had lots of talks on this."

Scratch a little more below the surface and you can encounter some haphazard planning, and sometimes a lifestyle which lacks a healthy balance. Ask the young person how they are coping and you might receive a shrug of the shoulders and a response like, "Fine". At this point pause. Have an open conversation linked to the effective management of time and what living a healthy lifestyle means in the real world of an adolescent.

I show young people my paper diary and how I plan my day, my time, and the tasks I must achieve by specific deadlines, as an encouragement to think more about their planning and organization—think: "walk the talk".

I also share how I learnt, through trial and error during my adolescence, how to develop an effective study schedule which allowed time for my sport and other interests. I seemed to have nine hours sleep most nights without fully appreciating its importance, and made sure I had a good breakfast before heading off to school.

Teenagers crave structure

The surge of growth which occurs in the frontal lobes, particularly in the prefrontal cortex of the brain, can lead youth to overcomplicate problems, idealize the world, and say one thing while doing another.

I clearly remember those days as a teenager. I was going to head out and rid the world of injustices and global poverty. Then I had to find a job, feed, educate and house a family, and, suddenly, these ideals were tougher than I had anticipated. What was important, though, was that the significant adults around me during these formative teenage years had encouraged me to dream big. Many seeds had been sown that impacted my career in different ways and at different times, and continue to do so.

An interesting point from brain research is that, despite their attraction and susceptibility to novelty, teenagers actually crave structure and organization. What is more, even though they

ORGANIZATION

complain about it, they genuinely value adult influence in their lives, most especially that non-judgmental, authentic cheerleader.

I have found, and there seems to be sufficient research these days to support the notion that boys especially appreciate clear boundaries. Psychologist and educator Abigail James points out that boys are "less able to delay gratification and to plan actions and are more likely to be impulsive and less polite."[1] As girls mature, they begin to use the prefrontal cortex for decision-making. We are reassured that by the age of fifteen *most* teenagers are able to make sensible decisions most of the time.

Neurologist and educator Dr. Judy Willis describes the highly cognitive processes, otherwise referred to as high order thinking or critical thinking, which develop in the prefrontal cortex, as

> . . . skill sets beyond those computers can do because they allow for flexible, interpretive, creative and multi-dimensional thinking which prepares teenagers for current and future challenges and opportunities. These executive functions would include planning, flexibility, risk assessment, informed decision-making, reasoning, analysis and delay of immediate gratification to achieve long-term goals.[2]

Willis stresses that these executive functions further allow for organizing, connecting, prioritizing, self-monitoring, self-correcting, self-assessing, abstracting, and focusing.

In addition, education specialist Tony Wagner—who refers to today's youth as the "Innovation Generation"—highlights seven survival skills he believes every student requires for their careers, continuous learning, and citizenship:

1. Critical thinking and problem solving.
2. Collaboration across networks and leading by influence.
3. Agility and adaptability.
4. Initiative and entrepreneurship.

---

1. James. *Teaching*.
2. Willis. *Understanding*.

CHOICES

5. Accessing and analyzing information.
6. Effective oral and written communication.
7. Curiosity and imagination.[3]

As you absorb all this information, it becomes easier to understand why *organization* is one of the key elements within the CHOICES framework. Perhaps you'll also appreciate that there are skills students need to be taught. They require guidance, coaching, and direction, which includes regular feedback—with positive and constructive messages included at all times—on how to develop organizational skills.

Good organization reduces stress

Furthermore, brain scans show that under stressful conditions information is blocked from entering the brain's areas of higher cognitive memory consolidation and storage. When this occurs, learning processes grind to a halt. We can sensitively guide and coach youth in different ways to manage stress, especially negative stress, as the stress hormone cortisol—"being like a delinquent roaring around seeing what trouble it can get itself into"[4]—is more easily produced during these adolescent years.

Andrew Fuller shares how cortisol lowers language functioning and affects memory. So, stressed teens struggle to share their thoughts meaningfully "reply in short phrases or monosyllabic grunts."[5]

We remember more of what we hear and read when we are in a positive emotional state. This again underlines how important it is to create an environment in which teenagers feel safe with us.

Paediatric neurologist Dr. Andrew Curran states that "Our emotional brain underpins everything we learn—the more you

---

3. Wagner. *Creative Innovators*.
4. Fuller. *Tricky Teens*, 27.
5. Fuller. *Tricky Teens*, 27.

have connected with another human being emotionally the more they can learn from you."[6]

When we share this research with teenagers, they can better understand the importance of effective planning and strong organizational skills, together with living a balanced and healthy lifestyle.

Reasons for anxiety and stress

I once asked a class of teenage boys and girls to create a list of all the things that cause them stress. I share some of their responses simply as a reminder that a variety of things occur in their lives at a time when they think with their amygdala—the emotional part of the brain—rather than the rational thinking part of the brain, the developing prefrontal cortex. Therefore, they often find it difficult to see and appreciate the consequences of their actions and decisions. This could increase their levels of anxiety and stress, producing more cortisol.

What created stress in the lives of these teenagers? Parent or family problems; bullying; peer pressure; not coping academically; trying to do too much; parental pressure; not getting along with a teacher; not meeting deadlines; self-image issues; friendship issues; social media issues—there are no real surprises here. Indeed, we can probably empathize when we think back to our own years as teenagers and the challenges we faced.

Tina's experience

When I worked with Tina during her final year of school, she struggled with anxiety caused by her perfectionist approach to life, as well as parental pressures to deliver high academic results. Tina worked incredibly hard and rated in the top three of her cohort, though these results were—through her own admission—obtained at a tremendous cost to her personal wellbeing. She admitted that,

6. Curran. *ThE LITTLE*.

while she wanted to do well, she was unhappy and felt under constant pressure. Over a couple of months, we developed a new approach to her life choices which resulted in a more balanced lifestyle and, most important, a happy young woman.

I remember the day a beaming Tina walked into my office and told me that, for the first time in a long time, she had completed and handed in an assignment two days ahead of schedule.

"Planning," she said, "has made such a difference."

"As has the fact, Tina, that you exercise regularly, have nine hours sleep a night most nights—not five or six as you had last year—and also enjoy more social time with your friends."

Later Tina informed me that she had made another important decision which had also reduced stress in her life. She had moved away from her more negative peers, and spent more time with positive peers with whom she had developed some friendly and encouraging rivalry. While they competed with one another, they still spent time studying together and encouraging one another to achieve their specific goals.

Organization and planning tips

How then can we guide youth to learn organizational and planning skills?

Let's remind ourselves that in the earlier chapters we developed a goal setting process, and considered the importance of a balanced lifestyle. Now our task is to guide youth *how* to manage their time effectively if they wish to achieve their goals and enjoy a stress-less life.

I encourage them to set off on this journey with an open agenda, willing to try different approaches until they find something that suits their particular circumstances. When they adopt this approach, they quickly appreciate that they have the capacity to change their circumstances, to solve problems, and to communicate their thoughts and experiences with others. They become more resilient with every choice they make.

Organization

On a sheet of paper, I draw up a rough timetable for Monday to Sunday, beginning each day at 7.00 a.m. and ending at 10.00 p.m., a reminder that they need at least nine hours sleep every night.

Then we complete this sheet and note how much time is allocated to school work, health and sport or extracurricular activities—hobbies and interests—social time, and family time which includes at least one family meal a day together.

Inevitably most young people discover that they have plenty of social time, waste a lot of time, and, with a little more planning and self-discipline, they can quickly make noticeable improvements which can also be woven into the goal setting activity.

Study after study states that multi-tasking degrades the quality of learning. Indeed, some research shows that the brain is not wired for multi-tasking. So, the discussion inevitably moves to the sensible use of social media, being responsible, and making smart choices.

Depending on the student's situation, I might go further and help them draw up realistic and achievable plans to meet assessment deadlines—as I did with Rachel and Tina—where they plan for the weeks ahead and work methodically through the tasks at hand.

I encourage the use of a diary (or phone calendar) to develop daily schedules. As already mentioned, I share how I have used my paper diary for many years, simply to show them that there are different approaches one can use, while modeling how effective a paper diary can be in one's life. As youth place more structures in their lives, they train their brains—lifelong learning—to manage their time more effectively, and discover how to prioritize and organize tasks.

I usually arrange a time, within about a fortnight after this initial discussion, for us to review how the planning is going, how they feel, what's working, what's not working, and what needs to be tweaked.

When they complete a task, I unpack the experience while it remains fresh in their mind, using questions like:

- What did you do well?
- What did you enjoy about the task?
- What have you learnt from undertaking this task?

Patience and a sense of humor are important during this vital part of the journey. Encourage youth not to create unnecessary stress for themselves as they try and make some changes in their lives.

The great lesson learnt from activities like this, and which teenagers have shared with me many times over the years, is that, once their lives are better organized and they are on top of their academic studies, they have more free time to enjoy the company of friends, and to pursue other hobbies and interests. This was one of the great lessons Paul taught me when I mentored him.

Paul's story

Sixteen-year-old Paul was a boarder at the school where I taught. He was always the last student to get up in the morning, and regularly failed to complete his homework and projects on time. Paul was a talented sportsman who did well at his sport, though relied more on his natural talent than anything else. His supportive parents were realistic about his efforts, or lack of consistent effort.

I coached Paul field hockey and cricket. When his housemaster reached a point of total frustration, he approached me and asked if I would be prepared to have a chat with Paul to agree on a positive way forward before Paul failed his exams, and placed his future at the school in doubt.

Paul and I had an interesting conversation. I asked him if he felt he was achieving his best in the classroom.

"No, I don't think so."

"Why is that?" I enquired.

"I'm stupid," Paul quickly responded.

"Who says you are stupid?" I was a little startled at Paul's response.

"Everyone."

"Everyone?"

"My friends, some teachers . . . ."

"Do you think you are stupid, Paul?"

"No."

So began the journey of guiding Paul to achieve his potential. He said he would like some assistance. We were off to a good start.

I suggested that Paul write down all the subjects he was studying. Then after looking at his previous year's exam results, he could set some *realistic* personal best goals with a focus on the grade he would like to achieve at the next exam.

I asked Paul if he felt he was doing well in his sport. He said that he had made the first cricket team and was pleased with that.

"I think you can do even better," I smiled.

Paul looked surprised.

"Absolutely! You have a lot of talent. How do you think you can improve?"

"Get fit," he said immediately.

"Okay, go and have a chat to the physical education teacher and see if you can design a fitness program for the next few weeks. Come back to me in a week with your academic aims and your fitness program."

A week later Paul returned. He had written out all his academic subject results from the previous year and alongside each he had written some new goals. A quick glance at these results showed me that he had aimed to improve in every subject by between ten and fifteen percent. He was shocked when I smiled, shook my head, and put a line through most of his intended goals.

"How will you feel if you don't achieve the 55 percent you have set for English?" I asked.

"Disappointed."

"How will you feel if you obtain 47 percent and you set the goal of 45 percent?"

He nodded.

"It's better to set small, achievable goals and then keep increasing the target in small bits, so that, for example, by the end of the year you might achieve between 50 and 55 percent. Remember, too, that you are trying to improve in six subjects, so you can only make so much of an effort."

Paul reset the goals to make them more achievable. His fitness program looked great.

From that point on Paul and I met at different times during the next few months to review his goals. Many colleagues—most notably his housemaster—and students commented on a changing attitude. Paul's "Wow!" moment occurred when he came third in the school's annual cross-country race. Suddenly people took note of his achievements and his self-esteem rose. Most people did not know that Paul had been getting up at 6.00 a.m. most weekday mornings (in winter!) to go on his training runs. This was a choice he made without any pressure from anyone else.

Author Carmine Gallo wrote that, "A person with high self-efficacy believes they can reach their goal and they take the steps required to make it happen. They work harder. They raise their hands more. They ask questions. They practice, get it wrong and try again." Paul became a living example of these words.

Paul passed his final school exams a year later. He achieved most of his more realistic academic goals. He played representative field hockey and also performed well on the cricket field. Best of all, about ten years later I opened a newspaper and saw that Paul had been named "Businessman of the Month". I think he had set up an import-export business of some sort after he had left school and completed further studies.

Reflections about Paul's story

By the time Paul left school he was definitely on the right path to fulfil his potential.

I am fully convinced that when students set realistic, achievable, and measurable goals, share them with someone they trust, and genuinely aim to achieve these goals, their lives change for the better, and their self-esteem rises.

ORGANIZATION

When a young person is serious about goal setting, a significant adult can also coach them how to effectively manage their time. The two tasks go hand-in-glove with each other.

One of the lasting impressions I have of Paul was when he told me that, once he became more organized, he discovered that he had much more social time. And, as we all know, most teenagers want to enjoy their social lives.

Neuroscience findings to encourage healthy living

Brain research highlights that our learning power increases when we pursue activities that give us a sense of accomplishment. Often this is linked to identifying and using our personal strengths.

Paul learned how to develop some of his strengths. His life was transformed. When, as a teenager, I made new choices and changed my attitude, I focused more on my goals, discovered meaning and purpose in my life, and my academic results improved immediately. Extra dopamine, which promotes brain plasticity—learning—was released as these experiences became more and more enjoyable for both Paul and myself.

One day a beaming Rachel, by this time living a more organized and self-disciplined life, walked into my office to tell me how she had "aced" a Mathematics test for the first time in years—a transformational moment during her goal getting journey.

Consider the work of two brain experts, educator Alvaro Fernandez and neuroscientist Dr. Elkhonon Goldberg.[7] Their suggestions on how to manage stress can be included within a CHOICES framework which considers how youth organize their lives.

Fernandez and Goldberg point out that regular exercise, which we'll look at in a later chapter, can reduce the experience of stress, depression, and anxiety; learning how to relax lowers blood pressure, slows respiration and metabolism, and releases muscle tension; cultivating positive social networks of friends, family, and even pets can help foster trust, support, and also relaxation—many

---

7. Fernandez and Goldberg. *The Sharp Brains.*

ideas here for us to include in discussions with teenagers to encourage them to live a healthy and balanced lifestyle.

When youth have a part-time job, serious discussions are needed with regard to the planning and organization of their time. Unless the part-time job is an important source of income for the family and requires a different approach, encourage them not to work more than a maximum of ten to twelve hours a week during term time.

In the digital age many of our youth say they have their plans on their iPhone, laptop, or iPad. Check these out with their permission, of course, and then apply the same principles we have considered in this chapter. I suspect you will find, more often than not, that they still require guidance on how to manage their time more effectively. Push hard to encourage them to "physically" write these goals and plans in a paper diary. It enhances the brain's positive growth.

5 SPIRIT OF MENTORING TIPS AND STRATEGIES

1. Mentors share their paper diaries, management of time lessons, mistakes they have made, and some of the life lessons they have learnt as they encourage youth to reach *their* potential.

2. Mentors are consistent and caring role-models who *never* preach values—they *model* values.

3. Mentors focus on listening with empathy and sensitivity at all times—eye contact (where culturally appropriate) and positive body language.

4. Mentors reassure youth that it is okay to fail when they step out of their comfort zone—turn this into a positive learning experience.

5. Mentors keep an open mind as they journey with a young person in a mentoring relationship, and continually discuss

ORGANIZATION

the importance of the young person becoming the best *they* can be. What does this look like? What does this feel like?

CONVERSATIONS 2 CONNECT

1. Let's look at the way you spend your time each week. I'll share how I manage my time if you would like me to do so.
2. Much has been written about how much TV or computer time should be allowed each day. If you were a parent, what would you say to your child (who is now your age)?
3. When do you feel tired and listless, lacking the energy to do something? Let's consider ways to work through these times in a positive manner.
4. How many hours of sleep do you have every night? Why do you think sleep is important for brain development?
5. Have you ever failed at something at school in recent times? How did you deal with it? What can you learn about yourself from the experience?
6. Are your goals genuinely *your* goals? How are they "personal best" goals? Would you like to revisit these?
7. What do you like and dislike about your school, or work, or further training (as applicable)?

Chapter 7

Interdependence

> Understand the human in front of you.
> Then you will improve their self-esteem.
> If you do this you will improve their self-confidence.
> And, if you do that, they will feel emotionally engaged with what you are doing.
> This after all is what 'Love' is all about.
>
> Dr. Andrew Curran

ANOTHER KEY ELEMENT WITHIN the CHOICES framework is *Interdependence*. The reason I place such a high importance on this element is because we should continually remind ourselves that our brains are wired for *face-to-face* relationships with other people, rather than only through computers or other digital devices.

The increasing levels of anxiety and depression evident in more and more teenagers—made worse by the 2020 pandemic—are a concern. I fear that, without wise guidance from trusted adults, youth will turn more and more to social media to understand what is going on in their lives, and that is often not the best choice.

Interdependence

Author Susan Greenfield writes that,

> Social networking sites could be viewed as a kind of junk food for the brain; harmless enough in moderation, but deleterious when over-indulged . . . A heavy reliance on search engines, rather than researching, could result in agile mental processing at the expense of deep knowledge and understanding.[1]

A lack of emotional warmth and interaction can occur when communication is limited to texting, emailing, instant messaging and blogging. In particular, those new to technology—the digital immigrants—notice the isolation and depression more.

Greenfield encourages us to pause and respond to two questions. Our responses will significantly shape the way we guide youth.

1. What kind of society do we want?
2. What kind of individual traits do we value?

Sue Roffey highlights a key point echoed throughout this book: "Positive relationships are what people really do seem to want in their lives—at home, at work, and in their communities. Nearly everyone wants to feel valued, connected and supported."[2]

Build resilience

Interdependence can become a transformative element in a young person's life under the guidance of a significant adult who identifies a young person's strengths, and discusses successes and failures. These conversations also contribute to the development of the young person's social skills.

Roffey states:

> Connected kids learn the relationship values of respect, kindness, honesty and trust. This gives them the great advantage in developing healthy and sustaining

---

1. Greenfield. *Mind Change*, 283.
2. Roffey. *Positive Relationships*, 13.

relationships in their lives, one of the most significant pillars of authentic happiness. . . . some children are never given the opportunity to feel bad, sad or a failure, so never have to learn how to deal with these difficult feelings . . . . Resilience means not being so affected by an adverse event that it overwhelms everything else.[3]

Andrew Fuller offers some important words of encouragement: "What connects us to others is love and conversations."[4]

And, it is also important, when guiding youth, to consistently show that we are *genuinely* listening to them. My research over many years found that one of the comments students make about many adults in their lives is that adults do not *listen* to them. An example of effective listening is when I reflect back to a teenager how I think they are feeling—

"So, Julie, you seem to be feeling angry . . . ?"

"No, more frustrated."

"Okay. Let me share what I think you are saying." Or, "Thanks for clarifying that. So, are you saying that . . . ?"

We show empathy. We are authentic.

Linked to this is avoiding the temptation to offer advice. Teenagers are smart and they approach you if they know you will give them advice when needed. You might feel encouraged by this, also feel trusted and valued—that's all good—but how are you guiding them to solve a problem—a lifelong skill—and make their own decisions if you offer short-cuts?

An important part of the self-learning and self-empowerment journey is to guide a teenager to work through issues and come to the realization that they often know what the solutions are. When they work out possible solutions and then come and discuss these with you, you are an effective wise guide on the side.

---

3. Street and Porter. *Better than OK*, 123.
4. Street and Porter. *Better than OK*, 129.

Pause and reflect

Let's pause and reflect for a moment on our personal life journey. Who influences and guides us? How many pearls of wisdom have been shared with us during face-to-face communication?

What takes place during these conversations? We learn to form impressions of others, make inferences about their intentions, gauge their emotional reactions, and adjust our actions accordingly. So much of the communication process involves tone of voice, facial expressions, body language, the pauses—all those subtle cues which cannot be learnt through social media, hence my belief that empathy is one of the most important values or characteristics we need to develop in our interaction with young people.

In addition—and this was definitely true during my upbringing—when we create that safe space or environment, we provide the security that the brain requires to feel safe enough to transmit messages to higher levels for complex thinking.

Learning and memory formation is severely hindered by fear. In a fearful environment, almost no learning occurs.

Educator and brain expert Marilee Springer reinforces how, "Modeling intelligence by handling situations in a way that empowers all students is necessary to build and maintain relationships."

Understand the emotional rollercoaster

Authors Maia Szalavitz and Bruce Perry, wrote in their fascinating book about empathy,

> Humankind would not have endured and cannot continue without the capacity to form rewarding, nurturing and enduring relationships. We survive because we can love. And we love because we can empathize—that is, stand in another's shoes and care about what it feels like to be there.[5]

---

5. Szalavitz and Perry. *Born for Love.*

Even though I have some understanding and appreciation for the roller-coaster of emotions teenagers experience, and their focus on themselves, I am a firm believer in sowing relationship seeds in my conversations with youth. So, I'll deliberately slow down a conversation and encourage a time for reflection by asking questions like: "How do you think your parents feel about this?"; "How do your friends or peers feel . . . ?"; "How would you feel if that happened to you?"; "How do you think your teacher or coach feels . . . .?" I quietly develop the growth of social awareness, an important life skill.

I have a golden rule quickly shared in discussions with young people. The statement, "I don't know!" is forbidden. I explain to teenagers—with a smile on my face—that they have good brains and need to use them. "I don't know", becomes an excuse not to think about something, sometimes because they don't want to share, and that's okay. However, I want them to voice that feeling to understand it's okay to share such thoughts, and also to learn how and when to be vulnerable. Most times, when I force the teenager to think, good comes out of the conversation that follows—an interdependent relationship is strengthened.

During conversations, we allow the thinking brain, or the prefrontal cortex—our conscience—which makes up about 17 per cent of our brain, to consciously process and reflect on information being gathered. Here short-term relational memories will be converted into long-term memories or knowledge.

This is why, as adults walking alongside youth, the *timing* of our conversations with them is so important. Displaying empathy in a nurturing environment is likely to promote healthy creativity, intelligence, and productivity.

Seeking an identity

These adolescent years are, indeed, a time when youth need to establish their identity, autonomy, and a sense of belonging. Yet, as we have been sharing in this book, it is also a time when youth struggle with their sense of identity. They are on this journey

Interdependence

towards self-reliance and independence. There will be times when they might choose to go it alone. And that's fine, as long as it does not involve life-threatening actions.

Daniel Siegel, writing about teenagers, states,

> Ultimately, we learn to move from needing others' care during childhood, to pushing away from our parents and other adults and leaning more on our peers during adolescence, to then both giving care and receiving help from others. That's interdependence.[6]

With their heightened sense of self-consciousness and all the other changes in their cognitive and intellectual development, the rapid physical growth, changes in sexuality, as well as the social and emotional changes, research underlines the importance of youth having at least three significant adults in their lives during their adolescent and young adult journey. And those significant adults do not include parents, so imagine how much more challenging it is for youth to navigate their way through adolescence if the family is not functioning too well, or if there is an absent mother or father?

Psychologist Jennifer Fox-Eades reminds us that

> ... children who have not had an experience of sensitive care in infancy, for whatever reason, are likely to be inhibited in their capacity to learn, to require more discipline and attention, to be impulsively and easily frustrated, and to have poorer relationships with their teachers and their peers. They are also more likely to bully and to be bullied.
>
> The good news is that every relationship counts. We cannot change early experiences, but just one thoughtful, sensitive, loving relationship, one adult who seems to understand us, can cause changes inside the most damaged child. And little changes add up. Loving teaching or mentoring can make a difference to the world and to

---

6. Siegel. *Brainstorm*, 4.

children. It requires courage and patience, but love is at the core of excellent teaching or mentoring.[7]

Build a network of support around the child

When I work with youth, I ask them who they turn to for support and guidance, other than peers. We discuss the importance of having some non-judgmental cheerleaders in their lives. I encourage them to work at relationships with grandparents, other relatives, teachers or coaches, in other words with people they can trust, and with whom they feel safe talking about their personal stuff.

I share with them, as examples, some of the coaches, teachers and mentors who have been there for me at different stages of my life, just to reassure them of the value these relationships have on this life journey. As I share this information, I talk about the importance of learning how and when to be vulnerable with the adults we trust.

Youth learn to appreciate that when they are not stressed by negative emotions, they can control the information which makes its way into their brain. I provide the guidance and self-learning tools to help them understand this. I coach them how to approach their learning calmly, with positive emotions, and a positive attitude—and how to keep checking in on these emotions. As they learn how to do this, serotonin, an antianxiety nutrient, calms the body and tells it to slow down.

I also coach them how to listen to their "deep inner voice" as they feel more capable and lovable. A growth mindset occurs and they become more resilient.

When youth are focused and in a positive or controlled emotional state, their executive functions in the prefrontal cortex organize newly coded memories into long-term knowledge more successfully.

---

7. Fox-Eades. *Celebrating*, 194.

Andrew Fuller writes: "High impact conversations are as much about a meeting of hearts as a meeting of minds."[8] We create positive and interdependent relationships.

Here are two stories about how my headmaster mentored and coached me in significant ways during my confusing adolescent years, which resulted in an interdependent relationship that lasted until his death from cancer when he was in retirement and in his 70s.

My teacher, coach and mentor

My high school headmaster had a positive impact on my life when he coached me cricket for a year, and later mentored me when I was a student leader. He could see the potential in me that I was struggling to see, yet he was also a tough taskmaster who would never accept a second-rate effort.

As a cricket coach, one practice on a hot summer's day is etched in my memory. After school we had a cricket practice for about ninety minutes. On this particular afternoon he decided that we needed to improve our fielding skills. We participated in activity after activity in this beating sun—no water breaks, just a group of fifteen-year-old students chasing leather cricket balls all around the field. He barked instructions at us, demanded a topnotch practice and, because we respected him and wanted to keep our places in the "A" team, we worked hard.

At the end of the practice, he sat us down in the shade and reminded us that, no matter what the conditions might be in a match, we should never quit. I never forgot that lesson and I am sure there were matches I played in later years during which those words motivated me to reach new levels of performance. I have shared that story with many teams I have coached over the years, a reminder that the spirit of mentoring includes the passing of the baton from one generation to the next.

---

8. Street and Porter. *Better than OK*, 134.

CHOICES

The second story occurred when I made an error of judgment as a student leader and thought that I would be demoted. In a moment of foolishness, I had thrown a pine-cone in the direction of an object being held up by some students on a second-floor balcony of a school building. Unfortunately, during the movement of throwing the pine-cone, my hand caught in my jacket pocket. Instead of the pine-cone hitting the object I was aiming at, it broke a window.

I walked with fear and trepidation to the headmaster's office to inform him of this incident and received a well-deserved roasting for a few minutes. Then, instead of demoting me, he gave me the task of writing an essay of 500 words about responsibility. He wanted me to think about leadership and what acting as a role-model means in reality.

Not only did he read the essay from beginning to end, but he also added his comments and thoughts to points I had made before returning the essay to me. I still have that essay.

These are but two examples, as mentioned earlier, of the positive impact a significant adult had on my life during my confusing adolescent years. I had such respect for this man, that I knew I could take any personal issues to him. He would listen. We would share thoughts and ideas. He helped me appreciate the importance of *interdependence*. He also had a fantastic sense of humor—a brilliant amateur dramatist—and reminded me never to take myself or life too seriously.

Do your best to fulfil your potential

One of my significant and life-changing "Wow!" moments was when I understood and appreciated my uniqueness. I stopped being concerned about pleasing others, chasing false dreams, and "living a lie".

I describe this moment best as the day I could look in the mirror and say: "I am lovable. I am capable." The seeds of these thoughts were sown during my school days, though I only fully understood the ramifications of them after teaching for a few years. I came to a deeper understanding of the importance of interdependence, teamwork, and knowing how and when to be vulnerable.

Today the majority of our youth appear to be heavily influenced by social media and the variety of platforms they can access. Most of our youth understandably want to be "liked".

Susan Greenfield described how personal identity might be constructed externally and refined to perfection with the approbation of an audience as priority, an approval more suggestive of performance art than of robust personal growth.[9] She wrote:

> Cyberspace status is now simply measured by how "cool" one is, how many followers and friends one attracts in cyberspace, and not by one's talents and achievements. Add to the mix the unprecedented opportunity for concealing the real self, and the possibilities for an individual never to feel at ease in meaningful face-to-face relationships are even greater: the answer is to retreat instead into the safe world of the screen in the quest for approval, having done little to earn it, and indeed not even existing in the same way that people do in the real world.[10]

Achieve Greatness—do your best

A few years ago, I coached a state or provincial under fifteen field hockey team which participated in an interstate tournament played over a few days. The team played two matches each day, and one match on the final day so participants could return home in the afternoon.

This team had a couple of above average players, though overall it would depend on genuine teamwork and support for one another on and off the field.

We played a couple of pre-tournament matches which allowed the players to get to know one another, and gave me an opportunity to try different formations.

9. Greenfield. *Mind Change*, 281.
10. Greenfield. *Mind Change*, 281.

CHOICES

Once we arrived at our lodgings—our base during the tournament—I set ten-minute interviews aside for each player to discuss with me how they felt prior to the tournament, what their specific role or roles would be in the team, the areas they could keep improving as players, and I shared my expectations of them as members of the team.

In the evening we met as a team to plan for the week ahead. I had shopped at a local two-dollar shop and purchased each player a small hand-held mirror. On the back of the mirror, I wrote: "Have I done my best today?"

I handed each player a mirror and asked them to bring the mirrors to our evening team meetings during the tournament. I challenged them to reflect on their answer to this question each day. If every player could say he had done his best on the day, then we knew that the team had given of its best and that was all that mattered. It was more important than the overall results. Each player would bring something special and unique to the team.

I also reminded them of my golden rule when I coached: "If you have nothing positive or encouraging to say on the field, zip your lips!" This included never chirping at the umpires.

Develop a positive team culture

All my life, thanks to the examples of my own school coaches, I had learnt the importance of a positive team culture; that the team is greater than the individual; we all make mistakes, though no-one deliberately makes a mistake during a match; always play hard and fair; be gracious when losing, and humble in victory. I witnessed many teams I coached over the years come from behind and win matches against the odds as they learnt these basic coaching guidelines which led to positive choices and attitudes on and off the field.

Anyway, the team began the tournament well and managed to win their early matches. When we gathered as a team in the evening to review our day, all the players had their mirrors and were given time to reflect on the question on the back of the mirrors: "Have I done my best today?"

Instead of players apportioning blame on others for things that might have occurred during a match, there was more fronting up to acknowledge a poor decision, a player not following the game plan, or an area that a player felt they could improve. Often one player would voluntarily offer a word of encouragement to another player. On occasion a player would tell another player not to be so hard on himself. The focus was always on the team effort, and I enjoyed the positive tone in all our meetings. This appeared to be a happy team.

Midway through the tournament, Logan, one of the best players in the team, started complaining and moaning when a team member made an error. He also started questioning umpiring decisions. I asked him to cease. When he ignored me, I pulled him off the field and substituted him. Playing the game in the right spirit and with the right attitude was more important than the result. Remarkably, we scraped a narrow win.

After the game we returned to our lodgings. Logan was sulking and telling team members he wanted to go home. I called him aside for a heart-to-heart chat. He was surprised when I opened the conversation by telling him that, if he wanted to go home, I would call his mother and ask her to fetch him. I did not think she would relish the thought of a two-and-a-half-hour drive, but Logan needed to appreciate that the team was greater than him.

We unpacked what had happened on the field earlier in the day. I asked Logan to share his thoughts and feelings before I responded and explained why I had decided to substitute him. I reminded him of his considerable potential, and encouraged him to take some time out and reflect on the words on the back of his mirror.

Logan shed some tears, though eventually decided to stay. I don't recall if he said anything during our reflective team meeting that night. However, Logan was a positive member of the team for the remaining matches.

CHOICES

The total surprise to me was how this team bonded and supported each other. There was a "never give up" attitude. The final morning arrived and they had already won the tournament.

The team's manager and I watched proudly as the boys collected their winners' medals at the closing ceremony. A memorable moment.

Post-tournament reflections

I am a firm believer in the importance of intrinsic motivation. Our evening mirror activity encouraged each individual to reflect on their own performances each day, go deeper into their personal make-up, seek guidance if they needed it, and try to discern the areas they could develop further.

Team members came to appreciate how effective a positive team culture was on *and* off the field. Their body language was supportive. Individual players rose to the occasion at different times. Every player contributed in some way and at some time during the tournament to the team's eventual success. And, we had plenty of fun along the way.

I felt privileged to be a member of this team and to watch these young players develop resiliency and a positive mindset throughout the week. I hope they still smile when they reflect on their achievements that week, and have kept their medal—maybe their mirror too—in a safe place to remind them of their triumph.

Susan Greenfield highlights three essential factors often overlooked in education, and certainly not necessarily inspired by the current cyber lifestyle. She listed these as having a strong sense of one's own individual identity (and to respect it in others); to have a sense of individual fulfilment, and to be useful to society.[11]

When I reflect on that hockey tournament, I like to believe that each player learnt something more about their unique selves. I also hope that, as they reflected on the question each day: "Have

---

11. Greenfield. *Mind Change*, 257.

I done my best today?", they took one step further to appreciate their uniqueness on their journey to achieve greatness.

John Wooden offered some words of wisdom: "Did I win? Did I lose? Those are the wrong questions. The correct question is: Did I make my best effort? That's what matters. The rest of it just gets in the way."[12]

Each player made choices, reflected honestly about the consequences of those choices within a safe environment, and took a giant step on the road to fulfil their potential. Many life skills were learnt that week—including the importance of interdependence to achieve a team goal—which would assist their personal development in the years ahead, and make them better team players in the world of work beyond school.

Prepare for the world of work

This chapter highlights the importance of non-judgmental adults in the lives of youth, and stresses the importance of interdependence for the adolescent's journey. Some of the research and work carried out by neurologist and educator Dr. Judy Willis[13] helps place all the key elements within the CHOICES framework into perspective.

Willis shares that the qualifications for success in today's ever-changing world will demand the ability to think critically, communicate clearly, use continually changing technology, be culturally aware and adaptive, and possess the judgment and open-mindedness to make complex decisions based on accurate analysis of information.

Her belief is that the most rewarding jobs of the twenty-first century will be those that cannot be done by computers. If this is true, and I believe it is a credible thought, youth need opportunities to develop their higher order, cognitive skill sets so that they can develop reason, logic, creative problem solving, concept

---

12. Wooden. *Wooden*, 56.
13. Willis. *Understanding*.

development, media literacy, and communication skills best suited for many of the unknown jobs of the future.

Susan Greenfield states that, "Creativity thinking cannot be purchased, downloaded or guaranteed, but it can be fostered with the right environment."[14]

Yes, youth also need to be entrepreneurial, innovative and agile, but little will be attained without the face-to-face support of significant adults in their lives. Furthermore, we continually remind ourselves that every young person is unique and, therefore, no two people are wired exactly. Experience shapes us all differently.

Through interdependent relationships, youth develop key skill sets for their career pathway or pathways—research suggests today's youth might undertake between ten and twelve jobs during their lifetime—and learn other important qualities like tolerance, a willingness to consider alternative perspectives, how to respect and value diversity, how to resolve conflict with a positive mindset, and the ability to articulate ideas successfully.

Educator and design consultant Ed Carryer said: "To me, empowerment means students can go out and apply what things they've learned to the problems that they've never seen before, with parts that they've never used before."[15]

We continually remember that the brain has the ability to change as a result of experience and interaction with the environment, so every conversation we have with a young person has the potential to be life-changing—a challenging thought. Indeed, we can remind youth that the *only* certainty in life is change, to encourage them to remain open to lifelong learning.

Further words from Francis Jensen also link to most of the CHOICES framework, as we appreciate how teenage brains are both more powerful and more vulnerable than at virtually any other time of their lives:

---

14. Greenfield. *Mind Change*, 258.
15. Wagner. *Creative Innovators*.

INTERDEPENDENCE

> Our brains are self-built. They not only serve the particular needs and functions of the particular individual, but are also shaped—landscaped—by the individual's experiences.... The human brain's unique ability to mold itself—plasticity, thinking, planning, learning, acting—all influence the brain's physical structure and functional organization according to the theory of neuroplasticity.[16]

Values

Not too long ago I read about a global study undertaken with 200 global thinkers of the time. Five shared values emerged among all of them: compassion, honesty, fairness, responsibility and respect.

How will our young people develop these values if we do not model teaching, coaching, or mentoring qualities and skills in our relationship with them? Or, if we do not communicate and model clear values which are "taught" *and* "caught"?

A former teaching colleague and long-time friend Dr. Gordon Paterson shared a powerful tip linked to values in an address he delivered at a school end of year celebratory function, words of wisdom I wish I had heard as a young person:

> In the mid 90's while doing research, I was fortunate to spend eleven days working with Jack Canfield, author of *Chicken Soup for the Soul*, in Los Angeles. I recall us working on how to create our day, a short process one could go through to maximize what one could get out of each day. One step in that process was to "Hunt the value." The suggestion was that you never know where that one piece of information will come from, that one lesson, that one piece of advice that will have a significant bearing on your life. I would encourage you to ensure that in your communication with your teachers, your peers and your parents, that you hunt the value in what they have to say to you. You have two ears and one mouth—listen with positive intent. It was my elder sister who taught me a long time ago to always look for the good in a person. It

16. Jensen. *The Teenage Brain*.

stuck. So, when you go to your least favored subject why not turn that time on its head? Look for the good in that teacher and hunt the value in that lesson.[17]

We provide that safe environment where youth are comfortable to ask questions no matter how silly they think these questions are. We offer the space for them to find the answers. As they do so, they retain more information—lifelong learning—and appreciate the importance of collaborative problem solving. They feel empowered and confident to take non-life-threatening risks—the power of interdependent relationships.

Hopefully, this chapter encourages you to keep developing your relationships with youth, even when they pretend not to want your involvement in their young lives. Be the difference in their lives, simply by being consistently present and know that they *are* listening to every word you say. And, remember, that more recent research states that by the age of fifteen a young person's sensible decision-making improves and, suddenly, all those conversations we have had with that teenage brain start to make more sense—maybe that is why that hockey team enjoyed a successful tournament?

5 SPIRIT OF MENTORING TIPS AND STRATEGIES

1. Mentors explore ways youth can develop teamwork skills, understand its importance as a life skill, and help them reach their unique potential.
2. Mentors help youth to build networks of support around themselves—a key development as they strive to become the best *they* can be.
3. Mentors explore ways to open doors for youth—a work experience opportunity, or a meeting with someone in a career which interests a young person.
4. Mentors make sure that youth feel safe and secure at all times.

17. Paterson. *The Boy*, 319.

5. A mentor seeks to name and discuss a young person's strengths as the relationship develops. This builds resiliency.

CONVERSATIONS 2 CONNECT

1. How many people are in your family or extended family? Who do you get along with best? Why?
2. Do you ever feel any family pressure to become the best person *they* want you to be, instead of becoming the best person *you* want to be? When does this occur? Shall we discuss how to positively respond to this situation?
3. How would you describe yourself to someone who doesn't know you?
4. What is one of your biggest fears of the future?
5. Do you have any pets at home? You are able to choose a special pet—not a cat, or dog, or bird. What would you choose? Why?
6. Who do you think you are most like in your family? Your mother, father, or grandparents, or another relative? Why this choice?
7. Who is the best teacher or coach you have had to date? Why? If you could choose any teacher or coach to guide you, who would you choose and why?

Chapter 8

Consistency

> In the end you are never going to be certain that you are on the right path. You just have to listen to the call and trust that it will work out. The path isn't clearly laid out. You'll be guided, but if you don't start walking you won't get anywhere. Start walking, even if you don't know where the path will lead.
>
> Mark Burnett

I HAVE TITLED THIS chapter *Consistency* as it is important for teenagers to live a balanced and healthy lifestyle. Further chapters will consider the importance of regular exercise and the value of service to develop resilient and well-rounded young people. We can look at the six other key elements within the CHOICES framework and link each of them to this element to fully grasp the importance of educating the *whole* child.

The holistic approach to teaching and learning recognizes the connectedness of the mind, body and spirit. It focuses on the preparation of youth to meet any challenges they may face in their life, including their academic career—learning about oneself; developing healthy relationships and positive social behaviors; social and emotional development; resilience; the ability to view beauty and experience transcendence and truth.[1]

In chapter 5 I shared the work of psychologist David Walsh who described adolescent lives as a time when young people are navigating a "cerebral hurricane without a compass", such are the physical, emotional, social, and intellectual challenges they face. Francis Jensen describes the teenage brain as a "puzzle awaiting completion" and encourages us as we move alongside youth: "The dynamic changes taking place in the brain are part of what makes the adolescent years an age of exuberance."[2]

Sean's story

A teenager's friendship groups can either positively or negatively impact their lives. I spent time chatting to sixteen-year-old Sean, whose life had been a wobbly roller-coaster for almost a year. Sean acknowledged that he would appreciate some guidance from me. He admitted that he had made poor choices, had mixed with negative friends, and wanted to get his life back onto a positive pathway. Indeed, the only consistency in Sean's life was inconsistency.

No surprise what followed—we talked careers, goals and drew up a plan of action. We agreed both to a check-in time to see how he was travelling, and to stay in touch via email [within the safe and secure school email system] if necessary.

I reassured Sean that his behavior was that of a normal teenager trying to navigate their way through adolescence. In his case, his desire to establish his identity, autonomy, and feel a sense of belonging within a peer group, had led him to increase his level of risk-taking and experimentation, echoes of Peter's story which I shared in chapter 3.

Sean identified a career interest about which he was passionate, yet quickly acknowledged that, without a change of attitude, he would not qualify for tertiary studies. I guided the conversation,

---

1. Hare. *Holistic Education*.
2. Jensen. *The Teenage Brain*.

doing my best to empathize while Sean made the choices—this is self-learning and self-empowerment. We talked about the consistent balanced lifestyle, and discussed adequate exercise, a good sleep pattern, managing his time effectively, and revisiting his friendship circles.

I encouraged Sean to develop more than one friendship group. When he made the decision to play more sport, he immediately acknowledged new friendship circles were being formed.

Sean began to appreciate that the *quality* of his friendships was considerably more important than the number of friendships he had. He also held the power to choose his friends. Furthermore, he understood that the changes he wanted to bring about in his life were determined by him. My role was that of the non-judgmental cheerleader.

Positive peer pressure

One of the strongest themes in youth research is the significant contribution of positive peer relationships to young people's wellbeing and resilience. A young person's level of social competence and their friendship networks are a key indicator of probable academic achievement.

Psychologist and educator Abigail James[3] shares how her research has shown that, for boys, competition helps academic performance. Even though teenagers should set their personal best goals, if some of their peers also strive to achieve personal best goals, they become part of a circle of informally competitive young people which is healthy, as Tina also discovered in her self-empowerment journey which I described in chapter 6.

Part of my strategy, therefore, with Sean, was to encourage him to move into a positive environment where he would feel good about himself, have more and more enjoyable experiences, and enjoy more positive learning and friendship experiences. He

---

3. James. *Teaching.*

needed to appreciate how positive brain growth occurs when he was spontaneous and having fun.

The brain would, therefore, release extra dopamine which would travel to more parts of the brain, activating additional neurons with other positive spinoffs also linked to promoting brain plasticity—positive interactions with friends, laughing, physical activities, and reaching out selflessly to others. As dopamine levels increased from positive experiences and interactions, and a more consistent effort, Sean moved into a better head space to achieve some of his goals.

Dr. Andrew Curran points out that "your emotional self is centrally involved in creating who you are," as the wiring together of nerve cells remain predominantly under the control of our emotional system. Dopamine release is predominantly under the control of our emotional or limbic brain, and we require dopamine release in our brain to learn anything.[4]

And then he makes a significant point, which enhances the power of interdependent relationships: "If you have made good emotional connections with the person who is trying to learn from you (or from whom you are trying to learn), you have dramatically increased the chance of them learning that thing from you."[5]

Francis Jensen adds: "Memories are easier to make and last longer when acquired in teen years compared with adult years. This is a fact and should not be ignored. . . . This is the time to identify strengths and invest in emerging talents."[6]

Sleep

Another important area Sean and I discussed was having at least eight or nine hours of sleep *every* night—a *consistent* sleep pattern—something many teenagers fail to achieve for a variety of reasons. There is much research available now highlighting the

---

4. Curran. *ThE LITTLE.*
5. Curran. *ThE LITTLE.*
6. Jensen. *The Teenage Brain.*

CHOICES

importance of teenagers having at least nine hours sleep a night. I remain amazed at how many of them do not have this amount of sleep on a regular basis, and then express surprise when they start wobbling, and have to confront a variety of challenges that often lead to increased anxiety and stress.

Sleep is a key factor in achieving positive academic results. In a survey of sleep habits of 3,000 Rhode Island teenagers, those with the most sleep obtained As and Bs, those with the least received Cs and Ds.

The brain needs sleep to recollect experiences of the day and to prune or dispose of unimportant information, lay down new learning, and process new information. We need sleep to regulate emotions. Basically, the brain needs sleep to grow, change and re-energize so it can function properly during the next day. Indeed, scientists have learnt that what our brain learns during the day is *consolidated* during sleep.

Jensen makes a key point: "As so much is going on in adolescents' brains and they are learning so much and at such a fast pace, teens need more sleep than either their parents or much younger siblings."[7]

Nicola Morgan says there is increasing evidence to show that our sleeping brains practice the things we do while we are awake. She describes how REM sleep (Rapid Eye Movement sleep), during which time our eyelids are fluttering, happens at certain stages during the sleep cycle, particularly when we are experiencing deep sleep and dreaming. REM sleep is particularly important for memory and learning.[8]

Jensen adds: "Sleep not only consolidates memories but also prioritizes them by stripping them down into their components and then organizing those components according to their emotional importance."[9]

---

7. Jensen. *The Teenage Brain*.
8. Morgan. *Blame My Brain*, 65.
9. Jensen. *The Teenage Brain*.

Develop consistent habits

During adolescence changes to the brain affect the biological clock, a cluster of neurons that send signals throughout the body and control fundamentally all of the internal operations, one of which is sleep. Melatonin, the chemical that is released to induce sleep, is now distributed in the brain about an hour later. The teenager, who strives to become more independent, have greater self-control, and possibly works late into the night anyway because of questionable management of time issues, has some real challenges to face.

Again, when we discuss all this with youth and collaboratively work out a new management of time plan, all will be well if they choose to make the necessary changes to their daily schedule.

And, by the way, there will be times when teenagers work late and get up early for school and, come the weekend, they might want to sleep for a long time. This is normal—let them do so.

Tracey's story

Tracey was in her final year of school and was one of the top students academically. She approached me as she felt she needed some assistance to lead a more balanced and healthier lifestyle.

The previous year she had obtained superb academic results and was now feeling the pressure to achieve these results again. She told me that, even though she had done really well, these results had come at a great personal cost. The stress had negatively impacted her health.

"How many hours sleep a night were you having?" I interjected.

"Probably about five during the pressure times."

"Well, therein could lie one problem," I suggested, "so let's focus on the organization of your time and how you plan, with at least nine hours sleep every night becoming a habit. We want a more consistent, healthier lifestyle."

I encouraged Tracey to explore different options. Eventually she found the strategies that allowed her to fulfil her potential without experiencing burn-out. Within a couple of weeks, she had moved to a place of enjoying nine hours sleep every night, and had started an exercise program, worked on her diet, and said she felt happier, and a lot less stressed—more dopamine explosions as she developed consistent sleep patterns and regular exercise times.

Nutrition

Proper nutrition enhances the developing brain. Andrew Fuller has done a lot of work in this area over many years. His work supports other research which shows that, where we pay attention to nutrition and cognition, memory, attention, stress and intelligence, there is a greater possibility of positive youth achievement.

Fuller stresses that, "Diet also dramatically influences our mood and energy levels."[10] As our brains run on water, glucose and oxygen, he is a firm advocate for drinking about eight glasses of water a day. This does not include soft drinks, especially sugary drinks which can make one sick and lead to the production of fatty acids. Fuller points out that the "bad foods"—simple sugars or saturated fats in excess—make one stressed. For example, the amount of sugar found in one soft drink boosted the adrenaline levels to more than five times normal levels for up to five hours later in a study of twenty-five healthy children undertaken by Yale University.

Try and encourage youth to eat a healthy breakfast and to ensure they have at least three healthy meals a day, avoiding the so-called "junk food" as much as possible. The "junk food" takes longer for the body to digest. It is not good to eat such food when one studies as the brain is unable to focus at full capacity. Fuller shares many ideas in his resources for managing a diet effectively.

Proteins, fats and carbohydrates are important for the brain to function consistently and properly. Complex carbohydrates like whole-grains for breakfast [and a variety of vegetables] are turned to glucose (blood sugar) in the body and are used as energy.

10. Fuller. *Tricky Teens*, 112.

Youth can learn that when they skip breakfast their brains are starved for energy throughout the day. This means they are unlikely to focus and retain key information, so learning is more difficult.

Risk-taking and inconsistent behavior

There are important conversations to have with youth at a time in their lives when they are more prone to impulsivity, risk-taking and reckless behavior because of the chemical changes within the pleasure-reward center of the brain. This risk-taking begins at a time when the brain is not ready to calculate and decide what the best option might be. And, continually remind yourself that the prefrontal cortex is underdeveloped which makes it difficult for youth to look into the future and understand the consequences of their choices, especially about the possible harm of risky behavior.

Francis Jensen places things in perspective: "Adolescent boys shave and teenage girls can get pregnant, and yet neurologically neither one has a brain ready for prime time, the adult world."[11]

Nicola Morgan states that "much research shows that teenagers base their decisions about risk more on how they feel now than on thinking ahead to what might happen . . . teenagers take longer to decide what is dangerous and what isn't."[12]

My many conversations with teenagers have looked at poor decision-making, inconsistent and inappropriate behavior, and a variety of lifestyle patterns. Often, I heard comments like, "I just wasn't thinking"; "I didn't think it would happen to me . . . "; "I had no idea . . . "; "I didn't realize . . . "

Morgan describes how teenagers make different decisions and have different brain activity depending on whether or not their friends are present when they choose what risks to take.

We have already seen that the teenage brain is particularly susceptible to stress, and there is more than enough research about

---

11. Jensen. *The Teenage Brain*.
12. Morgan. *Blame My Brain*, 89.

possible long-term or permanent changes associated with substance use, indeed abuse of all types—a lack of a consistent healthy lifestyle.

Drinking alcohol, for example, will have a very different effect on youth than on an adult, as the young person's brain continues to develop. Alcohol reduces neurogenesis, the ability of the teenager's brain to grow new neurons, and ultimately reduces how much they might learn later in life. Heavy alcohol use can impair adolescent function by as much as ten per cent—they can end up with more memory and learning impairments than adults who drink the same amount. Furthermore, the earlier a young person starts to drink, the higher the probability that they will either have alcohol problems, or become an alcoholic as an adult. Alcohol also increases the dopamine in the brain—this time in a negative way—making the drinker more likely to seek pleasure and take risks, some of which could be life-threatening.

Morgan points out that youth require less alcohol than an adult to get drunk, the effect is worse, and the brain never recovers from the onslaught. She also states, "people [who] say cannabis (a mind-altering drug) is safe are deluding themselves."[13] She highlights—and this also appears in other research—that it carries the risk of later mental illness, damages memory, concentration and coordination and, in the long-term, could even lead to schizophrenia.

Jensen concluded from her research that the risk of schizophrenia is between two and five times higher than normal in people who used marijuana chronically during adolescence—it also doubles the risk of psychosis.[14]

I recall a teacher sharing with a group of students involved in a school-based youth mentoring program, how, during adolescence, she had experienced a tough upbringing, made many poor choices, and had dabbled for some time with drugs and alcohol. In her mid-forties she said she suffered from concentration and memory issues, reinforcing these research findings.

13. Morgan. *Blame My Brain*, 98.
14. Jensen. *The Teenage Brain*.

The wise guide on the side

As adults, we avoid dominating or making difficult choices or decisions for youth. Instead, our role is to guide them through the tough choices, and help them see the possible consequences of their actions or decisions by suggesting or simply hinting what might happen.

Psychologist and educator Professor Toni Noble states: "Risk-taking may sometimes result in setbacks, but appropriate risk-taking also contributes to success and self-confidence."[15]

Encourage youth to understand the boundaries of acceptable behavior and the possible consequences of ignoring any parameters. Boys, especially, as a result of different choices open to them, appreciate clear boundaries more than they admit. Most teenagers appreciate the opportunity to negotiate these boundaries, an important part of the self-learning and self-empowering journey.

Open and honest conversations with youth who feel connected and safe can indirectly teach them how to step back from their fast world of constant change and take time to reflect. The impulsive choice, which they might later regret, is avoided. These conversations encourage youth to tap into their thinking brain, the prefrontal cortex, where memories are stored.

There are many ways we can encourage youth to develop a positive and consistently healthy lifestyle which are covered in my other books. However, we encourage the development of a constructive and positive growth mindset by the way we praise a teenager's *efforts* and their work strategies. That is the key point: don't praise their intelligence, praise their effort. Then we positively impact the teenager's beliefs about why they succeed or fail, and we contribute further to their development of resilience by identifying possible strategies to use when they face obstacles and setbacks. This leads to increased learning, more consistent behavior, and higher achievement.

---

15. Street and Porter. *Better than OK*, 57.

CHOICES

Special conversations, a lasting impact

As I reflect on my sporting achievements as an adolescent, I have many coaches to thank. They saw the potential I struggled to see. They always encouraged the effort I was putting in to practices or training. They would sit with me after matches and diagnose how the team had performed, my captaincy role, what I had done well, where I could improve—these were always positive and constructive discussions, and I was that sponge listening, learning and growing as a sportsman, and as a person. Without realizing it at the time, because I had these significant and caring adults around me, I was developing *consistent* and healthy behavior patterns, and learning how to bounce back from setbacks.

Francis Jensen reminds us, " . . . in the midst of all the chaos of the teenage years, adolescents are developing a leaner, more efficient adult mental "machine"."[16]

No matter what teenagers tell us, they require—and usually value, even if this is never expressed—guidance and limits, or clear boundaries. While an adolescent's rational prefrontal cortex develops, significant adults serve as the *surrogate* prefrontal cortex, the consistent presence in an often-confused young life.

David Walsh offers some words of encouragement: "Helping teenagers learn to fly with their feet firmly planted on the earth requires more than knowledge; it requires strategy. If adolescents are to survive and thrive, adults need to supply large amounts of three ingredients—connection, guidance and love."[17]

5 SPIRIT OF MENTORING TIPS AND STRATEGIES

1. Mentors and youth negotiate times to meet—be flexible. Mentors *consistently* turn up on time.
2. Mentors model what it means to live a consistently healthy and balanced lifestyle.

---

16. Jensen. *The Teenage Brain*.
17. Walsh. *Why do they?*

3. Mentors seek to understand a young person's fears and anxieties as best as they can. They explore possible solutions together and make sure the young person understands the importance of setting their own personal best goals to become the best person they can be.
4. Mentors understand that they are never expected to have all the answers. They are ready and willing to consult others and, where appropriate, with the permission of their mentee.
5. Mentors understand the importance of nine hours sleep every night for a young person's health and wellbeing, and consistently discuss this as youth search for meaning and purpose in life.

CONVERSATIONS 2 CONNECT

1. What are three qualities you believe make a great friend?
2. What do you have for breakfast each day?
3. Do you fear failure? When or where have you failed in your life to date? How do you feel about this?
4. What three things need to happen for you to have a really good day?
5. Think back to three years ago. What advice would you give yourself?
6. How important are the thoughts that your peers have about you? Why is this?
7. What do you do or say when you become angry? What makes you angry? Shall we share ideas on how to deal with such situations?

Chapter 9

Exercise

It's not about perfect. It's about effort. And when you bring that effort every single day, that's where transformation happens. That's how change occurs.

JILLIAN MICHAELS

THROUGHOUT THIS BOOK WE are reflecting on the social and emotional wellbeing of teenagers, by which we mean their capacity to manage their thoughts, feelings and behavior positively, so they can enjoy life, maintain positive relationships, and work constructively and consistently towards their goals—and achieve greatness.

Consultant Ellen Kumata reminds us of the importance of preparing youth for the constantly changing world: "The world is changing so quickly that if you don't think forward, by the time you figure out what is happening, some will have beaten you to the market. We need people who can think out of the box, see the future in a different way..."[1]

---

1. Wagner. *Creative Innovators*.

Exercise

Sir Ken Robinson encourages us to look for every opportunity to engage youth: "All students are unique individuals with their own hopes, talents, anxieties, fears, passions, and aspirations. Engaging them as individuals is the heart of raising achievement."[2]

The importance of guiding youth to lead healthy and balanced lifestyles is clear.

We are considering a variety of strategies and ideas to respond to some of the key questions teenagers regularly ask themselves:

- Where am I going?
- What is important to me?
- How am I doing?
- What is life all about?
- Who am I?
- Who is important to me?
- What am I doing here?

In the previous chapter I shared thoughts about how we can encourage teenagers to work and play—indeed just be as consistent as is humanly possible, while still having fun, chilling out with their friends, and remaining the unique individuals they are. Undertaking regular exercise is linked to living a balanced and healthy lifestyle. Therefore, the sixth key element within the CHOICES framework is *Exercise*.

The brain's response to exercise

Brain expert Eric Jensen[3] describes how our brains can and do grow neurons, or nerve cells, many of which survive and become functional. New neurons, he suggests (and his findings are supported by many others working in the field of brain science), are highly correlated with memory, mood, and learning. This process

---

2. Robinson. *Creative schools*.
3. Jensen. *A Fresh Look*.

can be regulated by our everyday behaviors. Specifically, Jensen says, it can be enhanced by exercise, lower levels of stress, and good nutrition.

Indeed, exercise is strongly correlated with increased brain mass and better cognition. There is more research emerging to show that neurogenesis—the production of new brain cells—appears to be inversely correlated with depression: running, or jogging for example, can serve as an anti-depressant.

Francis Jensen reinforces this thinking: "Within thirty minutes of exercising chemicals known as endorphins are released in the brain. These cause mild euphoria (no-one knows why!)."[4]

More specifically, physical activity is said to optimize the development of key areas of the brain like the cerebellum, the large structure in the back part of the brain that helps to refine, smooth and coordinate motor movements, and the hippocampus which is linked to the limbic system, the group of brain structures involved with emotion, motivation, learning and memory processes (sometimes referred to as the emotional core of the brain). The hippocampus helps us to remember people, places and events associated with a particular memory. As these key areas of the brain are being optimized through physical activity, strong memory pathways, which can be more easily recalled, are constructed while further development of cognitive processing skills occurs.

There is, therefore, great truth in the well-known saying, "healthy body, healthy mind."

Many teenagers, experiencing all the highs and lows of puberty, react differently to the challenge of regular exercise. When they understand how it enhances their brain development, they might show a greater interest. That has certainly been my experience with youth. Stress how exercise *is* good for them—for their heart, their muscle development, their bones and their brains—as it creates happiness and improved learning abilities.

---

4. Jensen. *The Teenage Brain*.

Family discussions

When my daughter was about fourteen or fifteen, she had stopped playing sport. Indeed, she undertook no regular exercise. As someone who had been physically active all my life, I struggled with this. I began to encourage her to do some exercise of any sort. I hit a brick wall, though kept sowing the seeds until one day I stumbled on an obvious solution. We lived about fifteen minutes' walk from her school. I suggested to her that, rather than amble to and from school, she undertook the journey at a quicker pace.

There was the immediate opposition to the idea. After all, "what would dad know about these matters?", but then she took up the challenge, felt healthier for it, returned to an active sporting life and now, as a mum of two young children, she still does her best to undertake regular exercise, and model a healthy lifestyle to her family.

There would have been some subtle pressure from her younger brother who was actively involved in sport at the time, and spent many hours with his friends skateboarding on the hill outside our home. He continues to lead an outdoor life in his mid-thirties.

This experience with my daughter provides a helpful lesson to encourage a young person to develop a consistent and healthy exercise pattern: do fifteen minutes of exercise a day which "begins" to have an impact on brain fitness.

For most of my life I have undertaken some form of exercise. When I stopped playing competitive sport, I played social sport. Then I decided to train for half-marathons (crazy, I know) and ran five Auckland half-marathons. Now, in retirement, I try and walk at least eight kilometers a day. When wet weather impedes my walk, I become grumpy. I love the outdoors.

The message to share with a teenager is that more and more research shows that, if they do exercise for at least thirty minutes every second day, and for at least two-and-a-half hours each week, they will feel fitter, healthier and, in all probability, handle the academic and general pressures of life more positively.

A positive role-model

The challenge for youth becomes greater when we model our conversation in our actions. So, for example, in years gone by I would drop into the conversation at some point that I jogged five kilometers every morning when I got up. If I was injured, I would walk the distance and I was really grumpy if I did not do regular exercise.

No teenager wants to be outdone by a doddery old man, so most responded to the challenge and took great pleasure in telling me how much more they were doing on the exercise front than I was—mission accomplished.

If the teenager you guide has special health concerns, they must seek medical advice before undertaking any physical activities.

Include an exercise program as part of the goal setting journey. This becomes a helpful reminder to the teenager that a positive attitude towards exercise is beneficial to a healthy and balanced lifestyle. And, when they schedule exercise into their "daily" routine, it quickly becomes a habit.

If a young person wonders what to do initially, encourage them to participate in a cardiovascular activity which causes their heart to beat faster. This might include running, walking, skiing, swimming, biking, hiking, tennis, basketball, netball, ultimate Frisbee—there are so many options.

Tracey's story continued

I shared a little of Tracey's story in the previous chapter and how, as a high achiever, she tried to reduce the stress in her life. In addition to reminding her from time to time that she will never be perfect, hence the urgency to stop being a perfectionist, we spoke about developing this healthy lifestyle. She had been attending a gym and sometimes went on a walk with her mum, though her exercise routine was irregular. When she committed to a more regular exercise routine, she acknowledged that she felt better,

Exercise

calmer when under pressure academically, and was maintaining the nine hours sleep most nights. If she couldn't have nine hours, she was having at least eight hours sleep a night. I could visibly see the changes in her general demeanor.

Molecular biologist and research consultant John Medina commented: "When combined with the intellectual benefits exercise appears to offer, we have in our hands as close to a magic bullet for improving health as exists in modern medicine."[5]

Teamwork

Better still if young people can become a part of a team. Not only is teamwork a sought-after skill by employers in the real world of work, but for the teenager it can also lead to a new circle of positive peers, higher productivity, and the development of group and communication skills. The "ideal" for brain health is to combine both physical and mental stimulations along with social interactions.

Some of my most memorable moments at school involved being a member of a team—winning sports matches against the odds; being a member of a positive leadership group setting out to make a difference, or facilitating a team reaching out to disadvantaged people, especially children.

Sheryl Feinstein wrote that "adolescence is a pivotal time in a person's development. The changes teens experience determines much about who they are—their work ethic, self-esteem, morality—and who they will become. This, in turn, shapes our society . . ."[6]

So, it's important that we play our small, yet significant role to build healthy communities.

---

5. Medina. *Brain rules*, 32.
6. Feinstein. *Secrets*, 165.

Stay flexible

I have often used sporting or extracurricular goals—even hobbies and interests—as a way to link youth to academic performance and the importance of making the most of their education opportunities, and it's this flexible approach that can be a crucial skill in developing meaningful relationships with young people.

At all times we create a safe environment that is conducive for problem solving and meaningful communication. Listen with empathy. Trust and respect develop. Youth feel comfortable. They learn how and when to be vulnerable and release emotions. Reduce tensions and encourage information to surface. During those conversations, keep sharing messages of hope, and a message that you believe in the innate competence and self-righting capacities of the young person you are travelling alongside. Share a vision of that young person which, for any number of reasons, they are unable to see during the confusing adolescent years.

James' story: "She'll be right."

When sixteen-year-old James walked into my office I did not know what to expect. I had not taught James, nor had I coached him any sport. All I knew was that his tutor was pulling her hair out in frustration, while James' mum was feeling helpless and at a loss for words.

James was a gifted basketball player, yet eleven months from leaving school, he was a serious risk of departing with insufficient academic results to allow him to move on to a tertiary course of his choice.

Francis Jensen summed up the learning I had to incorporate into my communication with James when she wrote: "Teenagers may look like adults, they may even think like adults in many ways, and their ability to learn is staggering, but knowing what teenagers are unable to do—what their cognitive, emotional and behavioral limitations are—is critically important."[7]

7. Jensen. *The Teenage Brain*.

EXERCISE

My first chat with James was fortuitous. Perhaps it was because I had played at a top level of sport when I was James' age, did little academic work, scraped through my exams and survived another year. Or, perhaps it was because my headmaster had advised my father in my penultimate year of schooling, that if I did not step up and produce better academic results I might not be at the school for my final year.

James and I quickly connected that morning. He was open and honest about his shortcomings, yet did not seem too concerned either. "She'll be right," was a typical Australian phrase to suggest that there was nothing to worry about, and that things would come together okay. James needed to open his eyes to another reality.

Chase the dream

I asked James whether or not he had any long-term plans.

"I want to earn a basketball scholarship to an American university. They pay all expenses, other than the flight costs. Then I want to play basketball professionally."

What an amazing goal. I asked James if he knew what the academic requirements were to obtain such a scholarship.

James had done all the research. I had already looked at his recent academic results prior to our meeting. There was absolutely no way he would qualify for a basketball scholarship with those results.

That became a bitter pill for James to swallow. He had to understand that, no matter how good a basketball player he might be, no university would be interested in investing in someone who could not cut it academically.

Small steps

Towards the end of our conversation, I asked James if he wanted help with organization, planning, and managing his time as he had significant school, club and state basketball commitments.

CHOICES

Surprisingly, and with no further reflection, James said, "Yes."

An eleven-month mentoring journey began, during which time we focused on:

- The effective management of time—through trial and error over a few weeks James worked out a program that would allow all the basketball training, yet also result in his academic commitments being carried out punctually and to the best of his ability.

- Accommodating James' needs as an *elite* athlete, as he was playing state basketball which took up more of his time. For example, instead of attending the school physical education lessons twice each week, he was allowed to spend that time in the library focused on his academic studies. I could check up on him in the library at any time. This I did on occasions. It was also an opportunity at times simply to praise his efforts—a two-minute conversation which I hoped would encourage him to keep the focus on those academic studies.

- A healthy and balanced lifestyle. We plotted James' week together and shared this information with his mother. I insisted that he tried hard to incorporate nine hours of sleep *every* night. It took a few weeks for James to achieve this, but he did and soon told me how it was transforming his life. We talked about his diet, building social time into his schedule, and accommodating his part-time job.

- James' part-time job had to be accommodated within this schedule. This part-time job was important because James was saving almost every dollar to cover a basketball tour to the U.S.A he hoped to gain selection for. We agreed to a maximum number of hours during the school term. He could pick up extra hours during the school holidays.

- James' attitude to basketball and how he approached training, his matches, and the good and not-so-good days.

EXERCISE

The journey

James and I enjoyed a positive relationship as we were able to laugh a lot, and James knew that I would be honest about what I perceived with regard to his attitude towards school and basketball.

Early in the relationship he admitted that he was not having nine hours sleep a night. He was often kept awake by texting friends at all hours.

I challenged him to leave his phone in another room. He said he was up to this challenge. We agreed to meet two weeks later.

Well, James fronted up as agreed. He looked sheepish and said he had not succeeded with this challenge which was "too hard."

"Ah, James," I responded with a smile, "you don't have the courage to respond to a challenge like this. That's pathetic. If I was your basketball coach, could I turn to you during a tough time? Could I depend on you to be a role-model to younger players?"

Nothing more was said.

Two weeks later a smiling James returned to inform me that his phone was now left in another room when he went to bed, he was having the necessary sleep, and was already noticing the difference.

James' academic work also started to show some improvement. While there were a few wobbles, for the most part he met deadlines, stayed focused in class and started to achieve some of the academic goals he had set for himself and shared with me.

Basketball

James was selected to travel to the U.S.A on a basketball tour during the Easter vacation. The team played a series of matches which were attended by scouts or agents from different universities.

A few months later an excited James informed me that he had received at least three offers from universities in America, one of which especially interested him as the university coach, who had communicated with James directly, was regarded as one of the best.

"Have you responded to the coach, James?" I enquired.

"No, not yet. I'll do so soon."

"And by that time, you will have lost the scholarship opportunity. If you really want this scholarship, contact the coach tonight. Even if it's just to say that you are excited about the opportunity and will reply more fully later in the week. It's your choice."

That night James telephoned the coach. His scholarship was confirmed. James' part-time work would fund his air ticket to the university. Thereafter all his costs were covered. All he now had to do was deliver the necessary academic results to enable him to take up the scholarship.

James had a clear purpose. He was motivated. I kept in touch with James' mother and all his teachers. James knew that he had a team of people supporting him and he was accountable to others for the choices he made.

Leadership

Some of our best conversations occurred when James achieved another of his goals and was appointed captain of school basketball.

We talked about the responsibilities expected of a school captain—behavior on and off the court; behavior around the school, as well as outside the school. I was subtly preparing him to start thinking about how a basketball professional (still James' dream) should be a community role-model.

James responded superbly. He watched other school teams play and cheered from the sidelines. He assisted with coaching when he could, and took pride in his appearance on and off the court.

I remember watching a match early in the season which did not go well. James' attitude wobbled. He dropped his shoulders when he messed up, and showed his frustration.

This led to a fantastic conversation about teamwork, leadership, perseverance, encouraging others, being gracious in defeat, persevering when things were wobbly—how to be a positive role-model with a good attitude while never losing one's sense of humor.

Exercise

I noticed the improvement in James' demeanor on the court as the season progressed. He became more willing to talk about the highs and lows of club and state basketball. He had learnt when and how to be vulnerable. I was encouraging a strengthened mental attitude. James' level of maturity and the encouraging way he responded to the challenges he faced as his resiliency continued to develop were impressive to observe.

The mentoring season ends

James and I set up regular meetings during the year, during which we assessed his progress against the goals he had set. This was a great opportunity to keep affirming his efforts and to discuss the choices he made.

Three weeks before James wrote his final exams, he popped in to see me. He left me with a treasured gift which I knew he had purchased with his hard-earned money, and also a thank you card.

James wrote: "No words can express my gratitude towards you and for your help this year. I honestly don't think I could have done it without you. Here's to the final stretch of our time together! With many thanks."

Special words from an extraordinary young man. James achieved the necessary academic results (only just, I might add) to take up the basketball scholarship in America. Before he departed to America, he returned to the school to coach one of the younger teams for a season. It was good to see him giving back after all the support he had received during his time at the school.

I contacted James towards the end of the following year after he had been in America for about three months. He had settled well and was enjoying his new life.

Footnote

Fast-forward to a few months ago while I was writing this book.

CHOICES

James contacted me on a social media platform, as he wanted to connect. He was interested to hear how I was enjoying retirement. I saw that he was in his third year since leaving school, had completed his course in America and was now at a Canadian university for a year on a basketball scholarship. He said his plans were to complete one year at the university and then move to another Canadian university probably to undertake a business degree after which he would aim to play professional basketball. The dream remains intact.

Reflections

James' life gained greater meaning and purpose when he obtained the basketball scholarship offer. All he needed was an authentic and consistent voice for an important season of his life. I had the honor and privilege to be that non-judgmental cheerleader.

James reached out and asked for support, at the same time learning how and when to be vulnerable.

James gained a deeper understanding of the importance of goal setting. After all, as I pointed out at our first meeting, what would be the point of playing basketball if there were no basketball hoops?

James worked hard as he learned how to manage his time, plan and organize, while continuing to develop his basketball skills.

James made many sacrifices to chase his dream. He could have used the money he had saved from his part-time work to purchase his first car, as many of his peers had done. Instead, he invested it in an overseas basketball trip that changed his life and set him on the road to achieve his long-term dream to become a professional basketball player.

James developed his leadership skills, became more resilient and learnt that it was okay to fail when he dared greatly. There was always someone to move alongside him and put him back on the path to achieve his dreams.

Exercise

The competition in the years ahead will be tough for James. He knows this. I sincerely hope that he achieves his dream and look forward to following his progress. Whatever occurs, he has developed a variety of skills and experiences, more academic qualifications, and increased knowledge about exercise and healthy living to forge a positive career pathway.

5 SPIRIT OF MENTORING TIPS AND STRATEGIES

1. Mentors model how an effective exercise program positively enriches their lives.
2. Mentors continually remind themselves that they are responsible for building a meaningful relationship with youth.
3. Mentors encourage youth to participate in fun activities and to laugh often.
4. Mentors focus on the holistic development of youth, as this leads to discussions linked to a variety of life skills and possibilities.
5. Mentors continually remind themselves that they are neither authority figures, nor a young person's parent. They are always the non-judgmental cheerleader with a heart that encourages a young person to become the best they can be.

CONVERSATIONS 2 CONNECT

1. Is there any sport or other activity you have yet to try and which you believe you might be good at? Why this choice?
2. You are allowed to change three "things" about yourself. What would these changes be?
3. How do you deal with stressful situations? Can you think of a recent example?
4. Are you more of an indoor or outdoor person? Why is this?

CHOICES

5. Do you have one special sport or other non-academic school achievement? Tell me about it? Have you won other academic or school awards?

6. What do you do when you are feeling sad? What cheers you up? Is there a special meal you would like at such times, or something else?

7. At what age should parents allow their teenage children to make their own decisions?

Chapter 10

Service

> If people are not living for a cause, a belief or a faith beyond themselves, they are not building character, resilience or realism.
>
> Tim Costello

Our final key element within the CHOICES framework is *Service*. This involves giving of oneself and not expecting any reward. This does not appear to come naturally to twenty-first century youth, whose digital footprint seems to imply that they are entitled to everything they want, and that instant gratification is also a twenty-first century right, even though this is not the reality. Of course, this is not true of all teenagers, though I suspect most go through a phase when this thinking dominates—after all, they are living during one of the most selfish periods of their lives, so these thoughts are normal. That's why effective teachers and mentors learn how to address the young person's needs *first*.

Sue Roffey provided an interesting perspective, linked to wellbeing and the need to build a caring community, when she wrote: "When many in a community feel positively connected with each other, this can lead to a level of social capital in which trust and reciprocity predominate and there is a greater chance of supporting each other to attain shared goals. The focus on 'we' rather than 'me' is in everyone's interest."[1]

Daniel Siegel wrote how the teenage brain changes during their early teen years and sets up four qualities of their minds during adolescence: novelty seeking, social engagement, increased emotional intensity, and creating exploration. He stresses how vital it is "to keep the lines of connection and communication open and to remember that we all—adolescents and adults—need to be members of a connected community."

Siegel continued:

> ... numerous studies support [the] idea that the more we help others, the healthier and happier we ourselves become ... When we bring our individual skills and passion and knowledge for the benefit of the larger whole, we are maximizing our chances of solving the world's practical and moral problems . . . . Perhaps we can simply think of serving the world, of helping the planet and other people one relationship and one interaction at a time.[2]

Philip's story

These are powerful and challenging words that remind me how sixteen-year-old Philip, who was close to failing before he set some new goals and changed his attitude, used his interest in health and fitness, guided by a staff colleague, to help younger students with weight lifting and power exercises. He thrived doing this and also ended up coaching younger students. This kept Philip active and positive, and earned him a prestigious service certificate during his final year at school. His academics improved and he received the results that allowed him to enter his chosen course at university.

1. Roffey. *Positive Relationships*, 145.
2. Siegel. *Brainstorm*, 303.

Service

Philip had undoubted leadership potential but was using it poorly and making unhealthy decisions. There were rumors that he might be involved in bullying. We had some open and honest discussions over a period of about three months. I became the consistent encouraging presence. Philip responded by turning up on time for our meetings and, at an early point, made the choice to improve his attitude, as explained in the previous paragraph.

As significant adults in the lives of youth, our challenge is how to shift the thinking of a normal teenager from an "all about me" approach to "how can I make a positive difference in my community?" mindset, as Philip did while he changed his attitude and developed a new mindset.

Judy Willis wrote: "The research is clear—attitude matters." She points out that students who are generally optimistic enjoy better physical health, have more success at school, flourish in relationships and are more well equipped to handle stress in their lives.[3]

Always the optimist

And the good news, Willis also shares with us, is that brain research has confirmed how optimism is more a *learned* trait than a genetic one. Thanks to neuroplasticity, our brains can be trained to have an optimistic perspective, the half-full glass approach as some would describe such an attitude.

An optimistic state of mind enables a mindful response to stresses and a down-playing of thoughts of failure, frustration, and hopelessness. Optimism breeds the expectation of success, which in turn makes it easier for youth to make the effort necessary to achieve that success.

One of my personal mantras, which I share with youth, is: "there is a solution to every problem, so let's look for the solution". You will be amazed at how students, when they unpack a problem or a challenge with adult guidance and support, come up with a

3. Willis. *Understanding*.

CHOICES

positive solution—this is both self-empowerment and the development of resilience in action.

One approach to encourage youth to think about how they can be of service to others is to ask them to give you examples of some of the things they are grateful for, or things that they appreciate. Or, ask them what problem they would like to solve in the world. Or, perhaps there is a wrong or injustice they want to make right—this discussion can reveal a passion which, in turn, can lead to deeper discussions about planning for the future. Life gains meaning and purpose.

As a young person embarks on this journey, with you alongside as the trusted, non-judgmental guide, the level of brain neurotransmitters is affected. This will include the release of dopamine towards that developing prefrontal cortex where reasoning and logic occur. As we have seen in earlier chapters, dopamine not only fosters contentment, but is also the key player in the brain's reward and motivation system. It will include the release of serotonin which contributes to the regulation of appetite, sleep, aggression, mood and pain, and norepinephrine which is important for attentiveness, emotions, sleeping, dreaming, and learning.[4]

Richard Guare and Peg Dawson remind us, too, that levels of dopamine decrease during adolescence and this results in mood changes and challenges with emotional control.[5] So, we can keep sowing the seeds of how to be of service to others, because when youth start to share and practice thankful thinking, they develop a more positive attitude to their education experiences and their brains become more ready to learn.

Judy Willis writes:

> Gratitude has powerful physiological effects on the brain—and body. . . . Experiments have shown that those who keep gratitude journals or lists feel more optimistic and make more progress towards their goals. . . . Students who practice grateful thinking not only have a

---

4. Willis. *How to.*
5. Guare et al. *Smart*, 27.

more positive attitude toward school, their brains are more ready to learn.[6]

Remind yourself how the teenage brain undergoes a number of changes, thanks to neuroplasticity. We remain alert to these changes occurring each time we communicate with youth. They increase their ability to express their feelings and emotions, and to communicate more effectively, while also expanding their understanding of the development of values, morals, and a sense of conscience. We promote optimal student wellbeing which Sue Roffey and a number of international experts in the area of general and youth wellbeing agreed is the desirable level of wellbeing for youth.

> Optimal student wellbeing is a sustainable emotional state characterized by (predominantly) positive mood, attitude and relationships at school, resilience, self-optimization and a high level of satisfaction with learning experiences.[7]

Mark's story

Mark wobbled badly in his senior school years, but, with guidance and non-judgmental support, he chose to embark on the goal setting pathway as he had some sports goals he wanted to achieve. The only way he could achieve these goals was to focus on the development of his whole being.

A colleague had complained that Mark was making unnecessarily judgmental comments about the indigenous people in Australia. They were silly, unnecessary comments.

When we were having one of our catch-up sessions, I simply asked Mark to pause and reflect as I posed a question: "Have you ever been without food, clothing, family support, and an education?"

Mark shook his head. No, he had not had such experiences.

6. Willis. *How to.*
7. Roffey. *Positive Relationships*, 19.

I asked him if he could even imagine what it must be like to be in such a situation. He admitted, as did I, that it was really difficult to imagine what such a lifestyle would be like.

Mark gained another free lesson about empathy, but I was also speaking into his leadership abilities by sharing with him that one day he might be playing sport alongside some indigenous team mates, for example, who might have had such an upbringing. His role was to be an encouragement, a support, and a genuine mate. He could take on these roles if he paused and considered where some of these team mates had come from. Maybe, as he came to know them, there would be an appropriate time for the sharing of life stories. The seeds of service were being sown.

At a later date Mark told me that he had thought about our conversation and the silly comments had ceased. This was confirmed by his teacher.

Share powerful images

With the advent of social media and the digital age, it is powerful projecting images, for example, of children suffering in poverty, or living in a refugee camp, or in war-torn countries. We can talk about situations like these with youth and ask them how they think they can make a small contribution to make the world a better place by starting within their community.

They develop a sense of "community", explore strategies to see how people can help each other, the importance of looking at problems from different perspectives, while also learning that life is not linear and there are a variety of pathways that can lead to one reaching one's potential, or solving a problem.

Sir Ken Robinson writes: "People will achieve miracles if they are motivated by a driving vision and a sense of purpose."[8] Our conversations—as I have shared throughout this book—assist youth to find meaning and purpose.

---

8. Robinson. *Creating schools.*

Service

I can share with youth how my wife and I, over many years, made a monthly donation to sponsor some children living in disadvantaged communities, why we did this, how I feel about this, how both our children took on sponsoring a child when they started part-time work as young students—that dopamine rush—and then discuss with them what acts of service they can undertake.

They might ask me further questions and I can share how a variety of fund-raising events when I was at school sowed the seeds for my giving of funds and my volunteer times in later years. At school we raised funds to feed disadvantaged children, and I remember organizing a variety concert at the school at which students from a disadvantaged community performed. Funds raised from this activity went back to that youth group to encourage and support them.

I learnt during these adolescent years that, during the times when I wallowed in self-pity, reaching out to others was an effective strategy to change my mindset and become a positive person of influence—not always easy, though *always* achievable if I *chose* this approach.

I shared Peter's story in chapter 3. Peter's house at school sponsored a disadvantaged child in another country. Each student was encouraged to contribute $8 a year towards sponsorship costs, preferably money they had earned carrying out one or more jobs—this would give them time to think about why they were undertaking the work. Peter voluntarily told me that he thought this was a truly worthy cause and he had no problem donating more than the $8 requested from money he earned in his part-time job.

Maybe we can encourage teenagers to become involved in a local environmental project, volunteer at a local RSPCA, offer to assist in a program feeding homeless people, raise funds for a worthwhile cause by encouraging their friends to join them on a sponsored walk, run or ride, or entertain the elderly at an aged care home if they have musical or singing gifts.

Make a positive difference

When youth share the ideas, we have the opportunity to support their selflessness as they learn how to use their strengths to make a positive difference in their community. The brain is strengthened and enriched with a combination of physical and mental exercises which also sharpen its focus.

So, we can guide youth sensitively on a journey during which they learn that little changes add up to big changes, and one person *can* make a difference; that generosity flows naturally from gratitude, since a focus on the good things we have tends to encourage us to feel we have plenty to share; and generosity is closely related to the strength of kindness, generosity benefitting both the giver and the receiver.

Leadership expert John Gordon describes what our servant leadership model can look like in our work with youth: "You serve others by investing in them: you develop them, encourage them, uplift them, inspire them . . . the more you serve the people below you [or those walking alongside you], and the more you empower and encourage them, the more likely they are to perform at a higher level and actually raise you and your organization to a higher level."[9]

Pay it forward

Tim Costello, former chief executive of World Vision, Australia, reminds us that service is about attitude. Instead of saying, "I am not just going to be good," say, "I *want* to be good." Costello states: "A global world demands a global citizenship, a global ethic, and a recognition that we have to solve most of the pressing problems globally . . . "

Expressed another way, Sir Ken Robinson writes: "As the world becomes more interdependent, cultivating compassion is a moral and a practical imperative."[10]

9. Barna. *Master Leaders.*
10. Robinson. *Creating schools.*

Service

Before I retired from my assistant head position, I taught a couple of classes. Over a six-week period, students were encouraged to undertake five random acts of kindness each week, record these in a journal which I provided, and, at the end of each week, write or draw an expression of how they felt as they reached out to others. Most important, I shared with them how these random, selfless moments positively impact their brain development.

Girls embraced this short project more than the boys because of their slightly advanced level of maturity, yet there were always surprises. Many wonderful and unselfish stories were shared as young lives were transformed.

Research also highlights how, through their participation in voluntary acts of service, youth continue to volunteer within their communities later in life. I saw the seeds of that happening in a few young lives in the years that followed the random acts of kindness project, and, as already mentioned, my life has always included an aspect of service, thanks to my school experiences.

When students become involved in acts of service within the local and wider community, you will be amazed at how most embrace the challenge. They reveal insights and observations that might positively surprise you. Coach them that they do not have to do anything extraordinary or wait for anyone else before heading out to make a positive difference in the world, a lesson that Ella reminded me of a few years ago.

Ella's selfless experience

Ella felt passionate about reaching out to some disadvantaged children. She and a friend, Abby, sat down and worked out a fundraising venture. They brought it to me. We costed it and worked together on the details. Permission was given. The activity raised $2000 for that cause and became an annual event at the school— Ella and Abby mentored the two students who ran the event the following year. Ella did not wait for others to take the lead. She had a passion and chased it.

CHOICES

Ella chose her own narrative, which embraced a message of hope and displayed care and empathy. She and Abby had to deal with the inevitable negative peer pressure from some of their more self-centered peers. This was uncomfortable, even a little confronting, yet Ella chose to share these deeper thoughts with me. Through our interactions, both Ella and Abby grew socially and personally. They also learnt many life skills: budgeting, planning, organizing, setting and achieving a goal, dealing with conflict, and the triumph of hard work. I am sure many dopamine rushes occurred in those two young lives during those months.

Ella continued to be involved in a variety of charitable services and activities during her university years.

The power of servant leadership

If you are a mentor, for example, you can discover how, when you undertake some form of community service with your teenage mentee, you model the meaning of selfless service. You also create wonderful opportunities to chat informally about issues your mentee wants to talk about, either while you undertake the service, or while you might be travelling to and from the place where you perform the service—feeding the homeless; helping out at a pet shelter; tidying up the garden of an elderly resident; playing games with disadvantaged or sick children, or coaching sport, dance, art, or music.

Jennifer Fox-Eades wrote how hope and optimism are

> . . . forward-looking strengths, a belief that the future will contain more that is good than bad, and that we can influence it ourselves to make good things happen more likely. They are not just *beliefs*, they are also emotions, positive feelings that feel good in themselves and which energize and motivate us. Also, beyond beliefs and emotions, hope and optimism lead to *actions* which will bring about desired goals.[11]

---

11. Fox-Eades. *Celebrating*, 162.

Service

Mother Teresa's life was a showcase of authentic, selfless service. She is one of the many examples of people who have moved out of their comfort zone to reach out to others less privileged than themselves: "I am a little pencil in the hand of a writing God who is sending a love letter to the world."

I continue to learn and appreciate how I am just the pencil and God is the author. I believe I have become more useful to God, and my relationships with young people have become more positive and more meaningful. My parents, teachers, coaches, and mentors taught me that I can't give something I do not have. Therefore, I must love myself and take ownership of the fact that I am capable and lovable. I continue to learn that how I care for others gives my life a deeper meaning and significance. How about you?

5 SPIRIT OF MENTORING TIPS AND STRATEGIES

1. Mentors model servant leadership and promote ideas encouraging youth to undertake community service—an important step on the journey to become the best *they* can be.

2. Mentors and youth discuss different styles of leadership and how a young person can positively influence others.

3. Mentors and youth explore positive and negative peer pressure empathetically and sensitively.

4. Mentors and youth agree on ways they will communicate during non-scheduled times.

5. Mentors are unafraid to express displeasure at a young person's behavior in a compassionate and caring manner—remain the non-judgmental cheerleader, always encouraging the young person to become the best *they* can be.

CHOICES

CONVERSATIONS 2 CONNECT

1. You have one opportunity to give one gift to everyone in the world. The gift can be anything at all. What would you choose?

2. If you could go on national television and warn people to avoid three things, what would you say?

3. What is the best thing you have ever done for a family member, or a friend, or someone else? How did you feel at the time? And now?

4. What issues or causes do you care about deeply, even though you may not always share this information with others?

5. If you knew you would die tomorrow at 6.30 p.m., what would you do now?

6. You have just won the $1 million lottery prize. What would you do with the money?

7. If someone asked you: "What does it mean to care for someone?", how would you respond?

Chapter 11

Concluding Thoughts: Make Sense of Confusion

> The plasticity of the human adolescent brain makes adolescence a time of great risk and great opportunity.
>
> Jay N. Gidd, M.D.

THE CHOICES FRAMEWORK REPRESENTS seven key elements within which youth, encouraged by non-judgmental significant adults, can focus during their adolescent journey as they strive to reach their *unique* potential.

The key elements we have considered are:

1. Clarifying goals.
2. Hobbies and Interests.
3. Organization.
4. Interdependence.
5. Consistency.
6. Exercise.

7. Service.

In reality, I have only scratched the surface. I have shared areas within which I have worked for over forty-five years as a coach, tutor, head of boarding house or hostel, teacher, school principal, mentor of teenagers and others, and developer of youth mentoring, and peer mentoring programs. I continue to learn as new research emerges and others share their experiences.

There are no hard and fast rules about how to reach one's potential. I have shared some of the most effective practices that I am aware of and still use today in my interactions with teenagers and those working with youth.

I use the word CHOICES, as my conversations with teenagers continually sow the seed that choices have consequences. Therefore, they have more control of their lives than they might fully appreciate, and, as the brain's frontal lobes mature, they are increasingly capable of moral reasoning and idealism. They begin to see the world through a different lens: "this is the world I see. This is how it could be."

JoAnn and Terrence Deaker make the point that, in order for the teenager to grow and thrive, their brains need three specific ingredients, though time and experience have the biggest impact:

1. Nourishment
2. Enrichment
3. Protection[1]

The CHOICES framework provides a multitude of positive opportunities for these three ingredients to thrive.

Richard Guare and Peg Dawson highlight the importance of interpersonal relationships in the lives of youth: "While on the one hand adolescents have a brain that is pruned for learning through experience, they also have a brain that is ill-suited for fully independent decision making about what those experiences should be."[2]

1. Deaker. *The Owner's*.
2. Guare et al. *Smart*, 25.

Concluding Thoughts: Make Sense of Confusion

Summary of key points from adolescent brain research

Some of the key issues from neuroscience research linked to the development of the adolescent brain which we have considered are:

- The brain, not hormones, is to blame for the often unpredictable and inexplicable behavior of youth. Francis Jensen explains: "Thoughts, feelings, movements and moods are nothing more than neurons communicating by sending electrical messages to one another."[3]
- Short-term memory increases by about 30 per cent during adolescence.
- The activities in which youth invest their time and energy influence what activities they'll invest in as adults.
- Youth are ruled more by their emotions than by logic.
- Youth crave structure and organization despite being attracted to novelty.
- Youth value the influence of adults even though they complain about it on occasions.
- Youth will climb the moral ladder only as their frontal lobes develop.
- Youth experience emotions before they can verbally articulate them. "Teenagers do more of their thinking and decision-making in the emotional parts of their brain."[4]
- Youth are more vulnerable to stress than adults.
- Youth are extremely vulnerable to addiction, and adolescent addictions are harder to break.
- Experience plays a significant role in the shaping of the brain—the neurons that fire together wire together—and can even change hormone levels and brain structures.

3. Jensen. *The Teenage Brain*.
4. Corbin. *Unleashing the potential*.

- Youth have trouble anticipating the consequences of their behavior because they rely more on the emotional amygdala than the rational frontal lobes—remember, the CEO area of the brain, the prefrontal cortex, is still developing.

I hope, as you have read this book, you have appreciated the important role of the consistently present wise guide alongside youth, especially when they feel aggressive, threatened, volatile and uptight, and why it's important for you to encourage them to pause and reflect before saying or doing anything they might later regret.

Create a safe environment

Encourage youth to sit quietly and count slowly to twenty with some controlled breathing. As they do this, the brain learns to develop and reinforce the "habit" of responding to their anxiety by focusing on breathing. They become more self-managed and mindful. The brain replenishes those neurotransmitters like dopamine, which is released when we think of pleasurable experiences, as we guide youth towards thinking of some recent positive experiences. This is why it is helpful to teach visualization as a key aspect of goal setting.

Again, given a scenario like this, it's critical that youth feel safe, secure and supported at all times. We create such an environment when they communicate with us. As we do so, we establish an environment of trust. The brain chemistry of trust involves oxytocin, the chemical that helps bond parent to child, mentor to mentee, friend to friend, or teacher to student. Oxytocin is also thought to lower heart rate and blood pressure, so reducing the activity of stress hormones.

We know too that youth remember more of what they hear and read if they are in a positive, emotional state when they hear or read it.

Daniel Siegel highlights the importance of "down time" in a teenager's day.

Concluding Thoughts: Make Sense of Confusion

> Downtime is when we have no plans, nothing we are trying to accomplish, nothing that needs to be done . . . a time designated to chill out, to relax and unwind . . . During this period the brain seems to recharge its batteries, allowing the mind to intentionally be given a break.[5]

Handle stress

The management of negative stress that causes so much anxiety, perhaps even a form of depression, is an important topic to discuss with youth at an opportune moment.

Highlight the importance of regular cardiovascular exercise; having between eight and nine hours sleep a night, staying connected with family, friends and significant adults in a teenager's life, and taking at least ten minutes each day for quiet reflection.

Keep promoting curiosity. We touched on that when we considered hobbies and interests—word puzzles, jigsaw puzzles, or Sudoku. Whatever the interest, encourage variety and novelty, as we remember that the ability of the brain to rewire and remap itself by means of neuroplasticity is profound. Tony Wagner stresses that: "Social innovation and social entrepreneurship are areas of rapidly growing interest, especially amongst those in their 20s."[6]

Dr. Arthur Kramer points out that "the ideal for brain health is combining both physical and mental stimulation along with social interactions."

Encourage positive self-talk, staying connected to those personal best goals which youth set for themselves; keep working at the development of organization, planning and management of time skills, prioritization (make lists); promote good nutrition or diet, and avoid multi-tasking.

Coach adolescents how to build strengths into their day and to look at life through an optimistic lens. Judy Willis writes:

---

5. Siegel. *Brainstorm*, 290.
6. Wagner. *Creative Innovators*.

CHOICES

> Brain research has confirmed that optimism is more a learned trait than a genetic one. We can train our brain to have an optimistic perspective, thanks to neuroplasticity. ... Optimism is easily identified in brain scans. Levels of dopamine and other brain neurotransmitters rise, cortisol levels remain steady, and the amygdala is open and forwarding information to the prefrontal cortex.[7]

The presence of supportive adults and a healthy functioning family are of critical importance when youth experience extreme stress.

Francis Jensen describes how, from her research, multi-tasking interferes with adolescent learning: "It takes anywhere between 25 per cent and 400 percent longer for a teenager to complete homework if multi-tasking." She describes how this can prompt the release of stress hormones such as cortisol and adrenaline. "Chronically high levels of cortisol have been associated with increased aggression and impulsivity, loss of short-term memory, even cardiovascular disease. Therefore, multi-tasking can wear us down causing confusion, fatigue and inflexibility."[8]

We are involved with the development of cognitive functions of the teenage brain in our interactions with youth. Cognition is linked to how youth understand and act in the world. Cognitive abilities are the brain-based skills they need to carry out any task, from the simplest to the most complex. Cognitive abilities have more to do with *how* we learn, remember, problem solve and pay attention, rather than with any actual knowledge.

Positive self-image

The focus in this book has been on personal development, and the beliefs about a young person's capabilities to learn or act successfully. Part of that learning involves the risk of failure and then, with the wise guidance of a significant adult, learning from that failure.

---

7. Willis. *How to.*
8. Jensen. *The Teenage Brain.*

Concluding Thoughts: Make Sense of Confusion

I haven't dwelt at any length on the impact—either positive or negative—of technology on the teenage life. It can and will be profound in the years ahead, and that's why my passion for working with young people stresses face-to-face communication as much as possible. Most people want to enjoy *meaningful* relationships with others.

Susan Greenfield makes the comment that "the more people are connected online the more isolated they feel especially when internet use becomes obsessive." She warns that obsessive gaming could lead to greater recklessness, a shorter attention span and an increasingly aggressive disposition, and quotes the results of a survey of about 2300 adolescents in England, Scotland and Wales by the British Charity Kidscape, where one in two adolescents stated that they lied about personal details on the internet.[9]

If you work with teenagers, you will no doubt have heard many stories about how they act differently online and create identities which allow them to be ruder, sexier, more adventurous and generally indulge in inappropriate behavior. As Greenfield concludes, "Time spent using technology is time spent away from the real world and real people".[10]

Francis Jensen promotes the power and importance of good parenting. Why? "Teenagers are vulnerable to the power of suggestion and there are a lot more suggestions now at their fingertips via the computer."[11]

John Medina advises that, "One of the greatest predictors of performance in schools turned out to be the emotional stability of the home."[12]

We must ensure that we, the "real" people, are a constant presence in the lives of the teenagers with whom we interact. As youth form their adult personalities, they need to express new thoughts and feelings out loud. Listening to them—as the non-judgmental cheerleader—with an open mind is a sign of profound respect. In

9. Greenfield. *Mind Change*, 127.
10. Greenfield. *Mind Change*, 151.
11. Jensen. *The Teenage Brain*.
12. Medina. *Brain rules*, 71.

the midst of taking the whole world extremely seriously, young people sometimes need the release of a good laugh. It is important for significant adults in the lives of youth to maintain a great sense of humor.

David Walsh sums this up well when he writes:

> The interactions between caring adult and growing adolescent are much like the connections forming in an adolescent brain. The more an adolescent has a diversity of positive experiences, the stronger connections form in the neural pathways of their brain . . . able to do, withstand and create. The connections between adolescents and adults who love them work the same way. The more we make, reinforce and re-create connections between our adolescents and the parents, teachers and other caring adults in their lives, the greater chance our children will have to sprout their wings and fly.[13]

Self-image falls within the self-efficacy framework and focuses on the teenager's neural photograph of themselves which they carry with them day and night. It's perhaps that answer to one of the questions most youth ask themselves: "What do I think about myself now?"

Resiliency

Strategies about identifying and naming the strengths of the young people with whom we work have been shared in the pages of this book. Once youth take ownership of their strengths, they start to appreciate that they have some key resiliency builders that will pull them through any challenge life throws at them.

What we can do—and these are some of the strategies I have shared in most of my work promoting the spirit of mentoring—is build a web of protective factors around teenagers. These protective factors, which foster resiliency, are characteristics of the teenager's environment that reduce the negative impact of stressful situations and problems.

13. Walsh. *Why do they?*

Concluding Thoughts: Make Sense of Confusion

The following six well-researched resiliency ways we can build protective factors around teenagers are the result of groundbreaking work over many years by resiliency experts Nan Henderson and Bonnie Bernard.[14] You can see how their strategies have been woven into the CHOICES framework and most of the brain research we have encountered (Appendix 2):

1. *Provide caring and support*—that is, unconditional positive regard and encouragement. This factor is regarded as the most important of all the elements that promote resiliency. It is almost impossible to overcome adversity or setbacks if teenagers do not have someone *consistently* "there" for them with the message: *You Matter!* Address youth by name; encourage participation especially if they are a little reluctant to be involved; investigate and intervene when they are dealing with difficult circumstances. Catch them doing well, and remember to praise their *efforts*.

2. *Increase bonding.* Strengthen the connections between youth and positive adults and peers (i.e., foster positive peer and adult relationships)—*interdependence*—and between youth and any positive social activity (e.g., sports, art, music, writing, dance, community service, reading, learning). Acknowledge the different learning styles of each young person. Encourage greater family involvement in each young person's life. What might this look like? Youth with strong, positive bonds are less likely to be involved in inappropriate or high-risk behavior than those without such bonds.

3. *Set clear, consistent boundaries.* Youth require clear and consistent rules or boundaries (e.g., family rules and norms, school policies and procedures, community laws and norms) within which they are encouraged to reach their potential. These must be clearly spelt out and consistently enforced. Encourage input from the youth you work with and guide. Negotiate with them over the boundaries and enforcement procedures (and consequences) with a caring attitude. In this

14. Henderson et al. *Resiliency.*

way they gain a sense of ownership, and receive the message that they are a valued community resource.

4. *Teach life skills.* Some key life skills are cooperative skills, entrepreneurial skills, positive conflict resolution skills, resistance and assertiveness skills, communication skills, problem solving and decision-making skills, and healthy stress management. These skills help youth to deal with peer pressure, and avoid pitfalls such as inappropriate sexual behavior, and drug or alcohol abuse. They also contribute to a positive learning environment because they help youth feel safe and secure.

5. *Set and communicate high expectations.* Expectations that are high and realistic are effective motivators: *I believe in you. I know you can do it.* Focus on a cooperative rather than competitive approach; involve youth in decision making: *You are valued. I value and respect you and your opinions.*

6. *Provide opportunities for meaningful participation.* Give youth responsibility by allowing them opportunities to solve problems, make decisions, plan, set goals, and help others—selfless service. Allow them to share power with adults in real ways. See them as resources rather than as passive objects or problems. Encourage youth to join school and youth committees, or positive peer programs.

The resilience champion significant adult

Whatever your role might be, you have the important task of coaching resilient youth to become the best they can be.

Richard Guare and Peg Dawson remind us that, "for [teenagers], anything that arouses emotion—fear of social rejection, the need to look cool, disappointing someone, disagreements with parents—can lead to less rational thinking ... strong emotional reactions from parents fuel the emotional reactions of [teenagers]." That's why the significant adult, for example, creates an important

Concluding Thoughts: Make Sense of Confusion

buffer between the teenager and the parent over an issue that typically might lead to conflict. "They play that vital role of surrogate frontal lobe (especially the prefrontal cortex) whose influence is gradually reduced over time as the teenagers become more proficient and practical in using their Executive skills."[15]

Always remember the importance of working on the basis of a developmental relationship rather than a prescriptive "I must save you", or "I can fix your problems", or "I will rescue you" attitude. Most youth will rebel against the latter attitudes, as the message you relay to them is that there's something wrong with them, rather than, "Hey, you're a normal teenager on this confusing journey through adolescence. I am more than happy to be an encouragement and support to you if you want me to be one of your cheerleaders."

So, here are some key qualities for the resiliency champion significant adult to develop during their lifelong journey working with youth:

- Show plenty of empathy;
- Express consistent, non-judgmental, and unconditional caring;
- Be an inspiration;
- Be trusting and able to be trusted;
- Be empowering and guide youth how to look at life in a positive way (Appendix 3);
- Coach and teach that youth have the power to create their own reality; they can take control of their lives by learning how to set personal best goals, even if these are initially small easy-to-achieve goals;
- Meet their emotional safety needs in a non-life threatening, non-abusive, or manipulative way;
- Be a good listener;
- Be compassionate;

15. Guare et al. *Smart*, 26.

CHOICES

- Be respectful;
- Provide a mirror and positive model of what can be obtained, which includes the important areas of sleep and nutrition;
- Be willing to be vulnerable, flexible, and honest;
- Guide them to understand the importance of taking time out from the internet, or texting, or social media to *talk* about any problems with someone they trust;
- Share true stories—YouTube clips can help as well—as youth can be motivated and inspired by stories of how others deal with the trials of life.
- Guide them how to look at potential conflict situations with a positive mindset. Judith Glaser states: "As you strengthen your relationship with others by listening and caring, you quell your amygdala and theirs, trigger your mirror neurons and theirs, create greater levels of empathy, and open your executive brain to thinking about conflicts in a new way."[16]

How do you respond to these two challenging questions which echo the thoughts of Susan Greenfield mentioned in chapter 7?

1. What kind of children do you want to raise?
2. What kind of society do you want to live in?

This book is partly my personal response to these questions. We probably will agree with Guare and Dawson's comment: "We want to see our children grow up to be independent, self-sufficient adults who make sound decisions."[17] Of course, you know by now, I would add the words "happy" and "interdependent" to that quote.

We want to encourage youth to reach out to others selflessly and to build community. So, we focus on teamwork. Businesswoman Colleen Barrett stated: "You have got a real team if everybody is working for the same cause and knows what his or her

---

16. Glaser. *Conversational Intelligence*.
17. Guare et al. *Smart*, 81.

Concluding Thoughts: Make Sense of Confusion

contribution is that will lead to ultimate success. In other words, everyone matters. You honor and respect everybody's contribution. You listen, you learn, and you lead others."[18]

If every young person can strive to reach their potential, and use their gifts and talents to take a message of hope into the world, the difference they can make can see a reduction in global poverty, the narrowing, perhaps even the disappearance of the gap between rich and poor, the end of greed, and they will become living examples of how the power of love conquers the love of power.

If each of us can be, as Mother Teresa expressed in such an inspirational way, a little pencil in the hand of a writing God who is sending a love letter to the world, what an amazing world we can live in. Be creators of a new post-pandemic narrative, and spread more messages of HOPE!

---

18. Barna. *Master Leaders*.

Appendix 1

Mentoring Matters

The material for Mentoring Matters—my community project set up in the late 1980s—has been developed in line with the findings of extensive global research about teenagers which I have conducted for over forty-five years. This research suggests that deep down most adolescents would like the following experiences:

To be cared for (loved)

- Youth wish to feel safe and secure.
- The more they are cared for, the more secure they feel.
- They wish to be surrounded by people who unconditionally care for them.
- They value the positive influences of peers and adults to encourage them to reach their potential.
- They are encouraged to appreciate that they are more likely to fulfil their potential when there are clear rules or boundaries in place (some of which can be negotiated). When they step over these boundaries there will be reasonable consequences.

APPENDIX 1

To be valued

- The more youth are valued the more positive self-worth they experience.
- They are encouraged to feel they have some control over things that happen to them.
- Empowering them is proof that they are valued, respected, liked and are regarded as valuable resources.
- They value fun time to interact with peers and adults, which also involves the development of social skills.

To know that life has meaning and purpose

- Youth want to know that they matter and their lives have significance.
- The more they understand that there is a reason for their existence, the more significant they feel.
- They value encouragement to explore opportunities within and outside of school to learn and develop new skills and interests.
- They are encouraged to acquire a commitment to learning: academic success and the long-term value of learning enhances their self-worth as they discover their gifts and talents.
- They learn to appreciate and understand how to make the tough decisions and choices, and how to cope with new situations.
- They value guidance to develop a positive view of the future.

These findings might help and encourage you, or be a useful reference point as you adapt the CHOICES framework at any point in the future.

Appendix 2

10 Habits to Reach My Potential

You can create a poster for a young person you guide and include these ten check-points which cover the CHOICES framework. These are proven tips or strategies that work.

1. Surround myself with positive friends.
2. Follow a hobby or interest during the next thirty days.
3. Exercise at least thirty minutes every second day—at least two-and-a-half hours a week.
4. Spend at least ten minutes a day reflecting on my life and purpose.
5. Get nine hours of sleep *every* night.
6. Join a youth, cultural, or community club.
7. Look for three adults I trust with my life (in addition to my parents), and stay in touch with them.
8. Give priority in my life to my school subjects or work.
9. Set myself Specific, Measurable, Intentional, Limited (achieve within a certain time period), Extended (out of my comfort zone), and Realistic (SMILER) goals which I know I can achieve with short and small action steps.

Appendix 2

10. Be myself. I am unique, I can have fun, and I will do nothing that could possibly be life-threatening.[1]

Happiness is a chosen state of mind. Look for the positives. Keep the focus on your goals. Make a positive difference in the world. Selflessly serve others.

---

1. Cox. *Letter*.

Appendix 3

168 More Conversations 2 Connect Topics

In addition to the Conversations 2 Connect discussion topics at the end of each chapter, here are more suggestions to help build rapport and connect with youth. As with any friendship or meaningful relationship, once the trust is developed, it is possible to communicate at a deeper level. Be patient. Be kind to yourself and display a positive and empathetic attitude as you connect with any young person.

There will be repetition in some questions. Other questions might not be suitable for the age group you teach, mentor or guide, so use wisdom and discernment when choosing a topic. Most questions will lead to different doors for communication opening. Be prepared for this. It is worthwhile to keep a journal of topics discussed during the mentoring journey where this is possible.

These discussion topics have been gathered from a variety of resources over many years. I salute and express my gratitude to all who have shared these topics.

The discussion topics have been divided into a number of groups:

4 Key Questions
26 General questions
56 Questions: feelings, friendships and experiences

Appendix 3

35 Career related questions
30 More general questions
17 Questions: deeper topics

4 Key questions

These key questions help build meaningful relationships, and encourage youth to feel safe and secure.

1. What are your expectations of this mentoring experience?
2. What role would you like me to play as your mentor?
3. Where have you come from? What is your life history to this point (only share what you are comfortable sharing)?
4. Share three things you have done in recent weeks which made you feel proud. I'll share three things I have done if you would like me to do so.

26 General questions

1. Describe a practical joke one day at school.
2. Describe a time when a message or conversation radically impacted or transformed your life?
3. Who is one of the most unforgettable people you have met? Why this person?
4. Share a recent situation or occasion where you were instrumental in the growth of another person. What did you do or say?
5. If there was one person in the world (living or dead) that you could spend a day with, who would this be? Why?
6. If you could choose to go anywhere in the world for ten days, where would you go? What would you do? Why this place?

Appendix 3

7. When you were younger, who was the neighborhood bully, or the bully in your community? What made that person so frightening? How did you deal with them, or respond to the situation?

8. If you could invite anyone to join you for a meal, who would you ask? Why?

9. If your house was on fire, what three items (not people or pets) would you try and save?

10. If you could have one of the following superpowers, which one would you choose: the ability to fly? Super strength? Able to become invisible? Why did you choose this power?

11. Who do you think are the two or three greatest musicians you know of? Why these people?

12. Which TV or movie star do your friends think is amazing, yet you do not share the same feelings? Why is this?

13. What is one of the great memories you have from your time spent with your family during the past two or three years?

14. People talk about heaven and earth. Do you believe in heaven? If so, what do you think it is like? Alternatively, what do you believe?

15. What is the most terrifying or scariest movie you have ever watched? Why?

16. You can choose your favorite pizza. What two or three flavors would you choose? Ice-cream to follow—your two or three favorite flavors? Oh, there is a soft drink too. Your choice?

17. Have you been on any memorable beach walks, or tramps, or special hikes? Maybe a school or some other youth group camping experience? What walks would you like to do if you had a free choice? Is there something local we could do together, or with a friend and their mentor?

18. If you could choose any three people to be your mentors or non-judgmental cheerleaders, who would they be? Why these people?
19. Who in your family or extended family can you turn to for support?
20. Describe your toughest life experience to date? How did you get through it? What did you learn about yourself from the experience? (note to mentor: see if you can identify and name one strength as your mentee shares. This could be a life-changing moment, which also builds resiliency.)
21. Shall we share our most memorable holiday experiences?
22. What do you see as the main problems or issues facing youth in your community? What can you and your friends, or you and I do to improve the situation?
23. What is your favorite food? Can you cook or bake? How about we teach one another a favorite recipe, maybe even cook a meal for your parents, or caregivers, or some friends?
24. What is your favorite dessert?
25. What is your favorite school or work lunch? Who do you eat lunch with at school, or in the workplace (whichever is relevant)?
26. What are your favorite magazines—either online or paper copies? Why these choices?

56 Questions: feelings, friendships and experiences

1. Who are you angry with right now? Why?
2. How easily do you forgive a friend who lets you down? Can you share a recent experience with me?
3. How old were you when you first realized that one day you would die? What caused you to think about death?

4. If you could change two things about the way you were raised, what would they be? If you come from a divorced family, how did it affect you?

5. Which do you value most: sight, or hearing, or speech? Why?

6. If you could wake up tomorrow morning having gained one quality or ability, what would it be?

7. What one thing have you learned about yourself during the mentoring journey, or during our time together?

8. How would you respond to this statement? Today, what I would like to change about myself is … because …

9. Under what circumstances do you feel most lonely? Least lonely? Why?

10. What is the first thing that comes to mind when you think about God?

11. Who is your closest friend today? Why this person? (Maybe there is more than one person.)

12. How important is your privacy to you? When do you prefer to be alone? Why?

13. Do you ever remember your dreams? Do you have a particular dream that often returns? If so, how do you feel about it?

14. If you could choose just one of these, which would you choose and why? Being super handsome or attractive? Having above-average intelligence? Being famous for doing something great, or for creating something special?

15. How many of your friends do you believe are honest with their parents most of the time? If not, what sort of lies or half-truths do they tell? Tell me about your relationship with your parents most of the time.

16. Imagine that you had a disability. Which disability would you choose? Blind? Deaf? Inability to work? Unable to communicate clearly?
17. What is one of the most memorable moments you have experienced with a friend? Or, something a friend has unexpectedly done for you?
18. Imagine you are in a scary place: on a boat in stormy water; an airplane in turbulent weather; a dark area where there is no light; alone in a dark, large building—what do you think or say to yourself during such a time? (You have no cellphone.)
19. Which movies make you cry? Do you think it is okay to cry at movies? What do your friends think?
20. When you think back over the years, and the good friends you have had, who were they? Why were they good friends? What have these friendships taught you about yourself?
21. How would you describe me to your friends? (the role can also be reversed)
22. Have you ever had a really scary dream that you can remember? What happened, or what was it all about?
23. Do you think about how intelligent you are when compared to your friends? What thoughts go through your mind?
24. What thoughts do you have about a good age to marry?
25. Imagine you could be someone else for a month and live their life. Who would you choose to be, and why?
26. Can you remember anything about your pre-school or kindergarten experiences? Three experiences—good or not-so-good?
27. Who are the popular students in your class or year groups? Why is this? What are your thoughts about being popular?
28. You know that a friend of yours has stolen something that does not belong to them. How would you react?

29. Which family member makes you laugh the most? Why is this?
30. How would you respond if someone falsely accused you of cheating?
31. What is the funniest experience you have ever had? Are there any life lessons you can take from that experience?
32. Which two or three friends do you think will still be your friends twenty years from now? Why?
33. What sort of things would you either like to stop doing, or do less?
34. Have you ever experienced or heard of the term 'positive stress', or 'butterflies in your stomach'? Let's chat about this and share our experiences.
35. Who are the people you share your deepest thoughts with? How easy do you find this? If it is hard, how can we work out a way to make this easier in the months ahead?
36. What are you enjoying about your job? (where relevant) What further training do you think will help your career prospects?
37. When do you find it easiest to communicate with your parents, or caregivers, or extended family? When do you find it hardest?
38. How do you express your anger? What do you do or say? How do others react? How do you feel about their reactions?
39. Who deals best with conflict in your family or extended family? What can be learned from their attitude?
40. Do you have hassles or challenges with bullying at school (or in the workplace, if relevant)? How do you cope?
41. Which unresolved conflicts are you still dealing with? Shall we consider ways to work through them in the months ahead?

42. You can marry any celebrity or famous person of your choice. Who would you choose? Why?
43. Are there any friends of yours you are concerned about at the moment? Why? What can you do to support them?
44. Is there anyone at school (or at work) you would like to get to know better? Who is that person? Why?
45. Would you be prepared to die for your best friend? Share the reasons for your answer.
46. How well do you get along with your siblings? When was the last time you had a strong disagreement with a sibling? What happened?
47. If you had to name one of your main weaknesses, what would you say?
48. Which is your favorite clothes shop? What was your latest purchase? How much online shopping do you do?
49. Do you receive a monthly allowance or an allowance of some sort? How do you spend it? Do you have a savings account, or ever think about learning how to budget?
50. What do you feel is your most difficult challenge or issue you are facing at the moment?
51. Which three things can you be grateful for today?
52. What would be one of your biggest regrets to date?
53. What is the most dangerous thing you have done to date?
54. What is the best compliment you have received to date? What happened?
55. What are the qualities or characteristics you would value in someone you wish to take on a date?
56. Who do you know who is gay? How do you feel about that? How do your friends respond to the gender issues?

APPENDIX 3

35 Career-related questions

1. What are your priorities at the moment?

2. How have you been doing in your school work during the past three months? Compare your results. What are your strong and weak subjects? What subjects do you enjoy? Why? What subjects don't you enjoy? Why not? What can we do to improve things for you?

3. So, you think your school work isn't great and you want to leave school? Have you thought about the importance of gaining the best education you possibly can for your long-term career prospects? Let's share some ideas around this.

4. Are you using a paper diary? I am happy to show you my diary, and we can explore ways of managing your time more effectively so you end up with more free time.

5. How much homework or extra study do you have? How are you handling it? Are there any ways I can support you, or are there any resources you need?

6. How much sleep do you get at night? When do you concentrate best in class, at work, or during your training (as applicable)?

7. Your examinations start in three weeks. Let's draw up a realistic revision schedule together.

8. Are you a member of your local library? When did you last go there? Would you like me to go with you? Perhaps we could check out what is in the library on possible careers for you, or your interests? If you want to join, perhaps I could help.

9. If you were applying for a part-time job, you will need a resume. Would you like me to help you draw up a winning resume?

10. If you could do any job, what would you be doing five years from now?

11. One day, if you could have a world-wide reputation for something, in what area would you like it to be? Why?
12. If you were going to leave the world one piece of advice before you die, what would you say?
13. What would your second career choice be? Why?
14. Name one person you admire (living or dead) who had to overcome great obstacles to get to where they are now? How has their story impacted your life?
15. Can you think of a time when you were part of a team that won something? What happened, and what made it so special? Any lessons from the experience you think could be useful when you enter the workplace?
16. What ability do you wish you had that you don't? Why? What can you do about this?
17. Which mentor—someone in a mentoring, or coaching, or teaching role—has had the greatest impact on your life to date? Why or how?
18. What career do you think your grandparents would like you to choose? A professional sportsman or woman? A TV or movie star? A famous explorer? A famous artist or inventor? A famous politician, or some other profession? What would your parents say?
19. Who is the best teacher you have had to date? Why?
20. Do you believe that men and women are equally smart? Why, or why not?
21. What do you do during physical education lessons at school? How important are these lessons to you? If your school does not offer physical education, do you think they should do so?
22. Do you have a cellphone? How much time do you spend on it? What about video games—do you play these? How often? Let's share ideas about the responsible use of technology.

Appendix 3

23. There is a saying, "honesty is the best policy". Do you agree with this? Why or why not?

24. Which famous historical figure has inspired you? How? Why this person?

25. What is the one thing you do really well most of the time? (It can be anything.)

26. You are in a basketball, or volleyball, or netball team. Would you prefer to win by forty points or six points? Share your thoughts.

27. You have been elected President or Prime Minister of your country. You have the authority to do any three things you choose. What would you choose to do and why?

28. A TV company has called you. You are given the opportunity to participate in any TV program of your choice. Which program would you choose? Why? Which character would you like to play?

29. How important do you think your schooling or education is in preparing you for your future career? Why?

30. Are there any issues at work you need to deal with? Do you have any strategies to deal with these challenges? (where relevant)

31. If you were made a teacher for a day, which subject would you want to teach? Why?

32. How many languages can you speak or understand? What are they?

33. What scares you the most about the future?

34. How do you respond to the statement that "money can buy you happiness"?

35. How effectively do you feel your school is teaching you the skills you will need to succeed in life? What skills do you think are important for your life journey?

APPENDIX 3

30 More general questions

1. How would you respond to this question (where appropriate): "If I could choose my career over again, I would choose ..."
2. What is your least or most favorite form of exercise?
3. What is your greatest personal achievement to date?
4. What has been the wildest prank you have ever been involved in?
5. When you were younger, what career did you want to follow when you grew up? What did your parents want you to be? And, now?
6. Where were you and what might you have been doing five years ago today?
7. You have just been offered a job at the local zoo. What animal would you like to take care of? Why?
8. If you could re-live one day of your life, which day would it be?
9. Can you name one thing you wish you had been taught when you were younger?
10. Can you think about a time when a team or someone won something and you were very proud of them? (you were not a member of the team)
11. Imagine I have to introduce you to a group of people. What are the five best qualities or things about you which you would like me to share?
12. If you could tell your parents never again to serve you two specific vegetables, which would you choose and why?
13. What is your favorite meal?
14. Have you ever been in an airplane or a helicopter? Are you scared of heights? Are you afraid to fly?

Appendix 3

15. Have you ever been in a sailing boat, or a motor boat, or on an ocean cruise? Share your experiences.
16. Do you have your own bedroom? If you could design it any way you wished, what would you do?
17. Have you ever imitated something you have seen in a movie, TV program, X-Box or computer game? What happened?
18. Many girls like to wear makeup. What do you think about this? How about boys wearing makeup?
19. Can you think of a really embarrassing moment in your life? What happened?
20. What age do you think should be allowed for a person to watch any movie of their choice? What do your friends do? How do their parents feel about this, do you think?
21. A friend gives you $1 million for a charity or charities of your choice. How would you allocate the money?
22. Do you have any household chores or duties to carry out? What are they?
23. Do you have a favorite restaurant? Why this choice?
24. What would be the weirdest or strangest meal you have ever had?
25. Would you rather live in the mountains, or by the sea, or in a city or town? Why this choice?
26. When have there been times when you wished you were either a few years older or younger? Why is this?
27. Would you rather be the owner (the boss) or the employee? Why?
28. You have the power to introduce just one rule that the global community must follow. What would be that one rule?
29. Would you ever get a tattoo? Why or why not? What would it be? Where would you place it?

30. How do you respond to the statement: "Students should be allowed to grade their teachers"?

17 Questions: deeper topics

1. When you look up at the sky, what do you think is beyond the stars? Would you ever like to visit the moon? Why? How do you think the universe was created?
2. How effective do you think the death penalty is? What do you think about the death penalty where countries have this?
3. When do you think torture might be justifiable?
4. What are your opinions about vaping and cigarette smoking? Should they be banned?
5. How do you respond to the statement: "Global climate change is man-made"?
6. What do you think are the arguments for and against Artificial Intelligence (AI)?
7. How do you respond to the statement: "Professional athletes, actors, and celebrities are paid too much"?
8. There are a variety of opinions about the legal age for drinking alcohol. What are your thoughts?
9. Do you attend a single gender or co-educational school? What do you think are the positives and possible negatives of these school systems?
10. How important do you think competition is in a child's education? Do you have any personal experiences to share?
11. How do you respond to the statement: "Animals should never be used for research"?
12. Do you believe we have a "throw-away" society? How do you think this issue can be better addressed—imagine you

Appendix 3

are a government minister responsible for environmental matters?

13. Should all governments provide free schooling and university (or post-school training), as well as a free health care? If so, how should this be funded?

14. Let's talk about our country's election process. What do you know about it? What age do you think should be the minimum voting age?

15. Do you think a lottery is a good idea? What are the arguments in favor or against a lottery? Would you buy a ticket for a national lottery each week, maybe even twice a week if you were allowed to do so?

16. How do you think photoshopped images might impact our thinking about ourselves? How do these images affect you?

17. If you were given a choice between home schooling or a school education, what would you choose? Why?

Acknowledgments

I AM INDEBTED TO my family and all my teachers, mentors, coaches, and friends who have guided me along life's pathways during different seasons of my life. This book is a tribute to *all* these people, too many to mention individually.

Many people have contributed to the content of this book. I have acknowledged most of them in the bibliography, though I have little doubt that some names have been omitted in error, as this book is a collation of many years' research. If I have inadvertently failed to acknowledge a source, I would be most grateful if the reader would inform me of this so that I can rectify the omission before any further printings of this book.

I especially acknowledge the work of neuroscientist Dr. Francis Jensen and resiliency expert Nan Henderson. Their work and thinking significantly informed and impacted my work, and enabled me to develop more meaningful relationships with youth.

Dr. Paul Browning, headmaster of St. Paul's School in Brisbane, Australia, read early drafts of this book and provided some helpful and insightful feedback for which I am most grateful. He also shared some words of wisdom with me after I told him how hard I find it to promote my books and my work. Paul encouraged me to change my mindset and to think: "I am not promoting myself but something I believe in. What I have learnt is worth sharing or it will be lost." Thank you, Paul.

I am grateful too for friends and experienced teaching and mentoring colleagues who offered me valuable feedback during

Acknowledgments

the writing of this book: Dr. Susan Weinberger, Andrew Cook, Lloyd Smuts, Dr. Sue Roffey, Hugh Huggett, Bill Gavin, Paul Fleischack and Fern Van de Pol.

Grateful thanks to Matthew Wimer and the team at Resource Publications of Wipf and Stock for all their support and guidance.

This book—indeed none of my books—would have been possible without the extraordinary healing gifts and talents of specialists, doctors, nurses and other medical professionals who journeyed with me over many years "dealing" with cancer. Never forgotten. You are *amazing* and *special* people.

My wife, Jane, and children Trish and Tim have encouraged me in different ways and at different times. They have tolerated my nonsense, laughed politely at my "dad jokes", and helped shape me into the person I have become. No words can adequately express my eternal love and gratitude to them.

Finally, sincere thanks to you for reading this book. Thank you for your care and interest in the wellbeing of our talented youth—our future. May all that you do motivate and inspire them to make the best CHOICES.

Bibliography

Barna, George. *Master Leaders*. Barna. 2008.
BrainyQuote. https://www.brainyquote.com
Brock, Sharon. *Stilling the Mind: An interview with Linda Lantieri*. Sourced from: https://www.edutopia.org. August 13 2008.
Corbin, Barry. *Unleashing the Potential of the Teenage Brain: Ten Powerful Ideas*. Corwin. 2008.
Cox, Robin. 234 *Discussion Topics and More Tips and Strategies to Encourage Youth*. The Spirit of Mentoring series (ebooks). 2021.
———. *Letter 2 a Teen—Becoming the Best I can Be*. Essential Resources (updated). 2016.
———. *The Mentoring Spirit of the Teacher: Inspiration, Support and Guidance for Aspiring and Practising Teacher-Mentors*. Essential Resources (updated). 2016.
———. *The Spirit of Mentoring: A Manual for Adult Volunteers*. Essential Resources (updated). 2016.
Curran, Andrew. *ThE LITTLE Book of BIG STUFF ABouT ThE BrAIN*. Crown House. 2008.
Deak, JoAnne and Terrence Deak. *The Owner's Manual for Driving Your Adolescent Brain*. Little Pickle. 2013.
Feinstein, Sheryl. *Secrets of the Teenage Brain: Research-Based Strategies for Reaching and Teaching Today's Adolescents*. Corwin (second edition). 2009.
Fernandes, Alvaro and Elkhonon Goldberg. *The Sharp Brains Guide to Brain Fitness*. William Morrow. 2010.
Fontaine, Claire and Mia Fontaine. *Comeback—a mother and daughter's journey through hell and back*. Regan. 2006.
Fox-Eades, Jennifer. *Celebrating Strengths—Building Strengths-based Schools*. CAPP. 2005.
Fuller, Andrew. *Tricky Teens: How to create a great relationship with your Teen … without growing crazy!* Finch. 2014.
Garringer, Michael and Linda Jucovy. *Building Relationships: A guide for New Mentors*. Hamilton Fish Institute on School and Community Violence

Bibliography

and The National Mentoring Center at Northwest Regional Educational Laboratory. Revised September 2007.

Glaser, Judith. *Conversational Intelligence. How Great Leaders Build Trust and Get Extraordinary Results*. Bibliomotion. 2014.

Greenfield, Susan. *Mind Change. How Digital Technologies are Leaving Their Mark on Our Brains*. Random. 2015.

Guare, Richard, et al. *Smart but Scattered Teens*. Guildford. 2013.

Hare, John. *Holistic Education: An Interpretation for teachers in the IB Programs*. International Baccalaureate Organization. 2010.

Henderson, Nan, et al. *Resiliency in Action. Practical Ideas for Overcoming Risks and Building Strengths in Youth, Families, and Communities*. Resiliency in Action Inc. 2007.

James, Abigail. *Teaching the Male Brain. How Boys Think, Feel and Learn in School*. Corwin. 2007.

Jensen, Eric P. *A Fresh look at Brain-Based Education*. Teachers Net Gazette. October 2008.

Jensen, Eric P. and Caroline Snider. *Turnaround Tools for the Teenage Brain—Helping Underperforming Students Become Lifelong Learners*. Jossey-Bass. 2013.

Jensen, Francis E. and Amy Nutt. *The Teenage Brain: A Neuroscientist's Survival to Raising Adolescents and Young Adults*. Harper. 2016.

Kulman, Randy. *Train your Brain to Success: A Teenager's Guide to Executive Functions*. Specialty. 2012.

Medina, John. *Brain Rules: 12 Principles for surviving and thriving at work, home, and school*. Scribe. 2014.

Morgan, Nicola. *Blame My Brain: The Amazing Teenage Brain revealed*. Walker. 2013.

Paterson, Gordon D. *A Boy from Mooi River: Growing up at Weston Agricultural College*. Ad Rem. 2020.

Robinson, Ken and Lou Aronica. *Creative Schools: Revolutionary Education from the Ground Up*. Penguin. 2016.

Roffey, Sue, ed. *Positive Relationships: Evidence based practice across the world*. Springer. 2013.

Search Institute. *Developmental Relationships Framework*. Sourced from: https://www.search-institute.org

Siegel, Daniel. *Brainstorm: The Power and Purpose of the Teenage Brain (an inside-out guide to the emerging adolescent mind, ages 12 - 24)*. Scribe. 2014.

Street, Helen and Neil Porter, ed. *Better than OK: Helping young people to flourish at school and beyond*. Freemantle. 2014.

Szalavitz, Maia and Bruce D. Perry. *Born for Love–Why Empathy Is Essential and Endangered*. William Morrow. 2011.

Van de Pol, Fern. *Correspondence with Robin Cox*. 11 April 2021.

Wagner, Tony. *Creative Innovators. The Making of Young People who will change the World*. Scribner. 2012.

Bibliography

Walsh, David. *Why Do They Act That Way? A Survival Guide to the Adolescent Brain for You and Your Teen.* Free Press. 2004.

Weinberger, Susan. *Correspondence with Robin Cox.* 8 March 2021.

Willis, Judy. *How to rewire your burned-out brain: Tips from a Neurologist.* Edutopia. 22 May 2012.

———. *Understanding How the Brain Thinks.* Edutopia. 2011/12.

Wooden, John with Steve Jamison. *Wooden: A Lifetime of Observations and Reflections On and Off the Court.* McGraw-Hill.1997.

www.ingramcontent.com/pod-product-compliance
Lightning Source LLC
Chambersburg PA
CBHW072134160426
43197CB00012B/2102